FREESTYLE SKIING

FREESTYLE

JOHN MOHAN
WALT HILTNER
BRUCE BARTHEL
Photographer

SKING
the
fundamentals

Winchester Press

ACKNOWLEDGMENTS

For their support and assistance in making *Freestyle Skiing, the Fundamentals* possible.

Dave Bossard
Scott Brooksbank
Jeff Brons
Crystal Mountain Ski Area
Elkhorn, Sun Valley
Joe Flick
Marsha Flynn
Dr. Ellen Kreighbaum
Dennis McCormick
Tim McFerron
Dr. Charles Pond
Carol Rush
Jim Sabol
Dr. Robert Schwarzkopf
Phil Sifferman
Diane Smoot
Lee Spingelt
Jim Tryon
Dr. Juris Vagners
Mike Vowels
Laurance Wieder

Cover photograph: Scott Brooksbank, World Freestyle Champion (1972, 1975, 1976) performing a Full Twisting Back Somersault (Moebius).

Library of Congress Cataloging in Publication Data

Mohan, John.
    Freestyle skiing.

    Bibliography: p.
    Includes index.
    1. Ski acrobatics.   I. Hiltner, Walt, joint author.
II. Title.
GV854.9.A25M63   796.9'3   76-25825
ISBN 0-87691-185-8

Published by Winchester Press
205 East 42nd Street
New York 10017

Printed in the United States of America

WINCHESTER is a Trademark of Olin Corporation used by Winchester Press, Inc. under authority and control of the Trademark Proprietor.

Book Design by Elaine Golt Gongora

DEDICATION
To our families and friends
and particularly Dr. Norman F. Kunde

Thanks for sharing a part
of your busy lives with us.
We deeply appreciate
your encouragement and guidance.
John Mohan and Walt Hiltner

CONTENTS

PREFACE

Since the beginning of modern Alpine skiing in the early 1900s, the skiing public has been influenced by national ski school techniques and by the national–international racing techniques used by Alpine competitors. Most skiers aspired to the "finished form" parallel turns taught by most ski schools, or to racing down a prepared course at a high rate of speed.

Suddenly, in the last few years, a new perspective has appeared—Freestyle. No other development in the history of Alpine skiing has had as profound and far-reaching impact on the technique, equipment, or philosophy of skiing. Because Freestyle did not evolve from national ski school techniques and progressions or in the arenas of Alpine competition, little information is available on the fundamentals of teaching or learning this new, exciting approach to the sport.

This volume provides a basic foundation in the fundamental skills and maneuvers, which may serve as the starting point for students, instructors, and Freestyle competitors interested in improving their skills quickly, efficiently, and safely. Because many of the funda-

mentals presented here also serve as building blocks for the skills required in the execution of the more traditional ski turns, an individual not directly interested in Freestyle can benefit from careful study of this book.

Freestyle skiing, originally known as "Hot Dog Skiing," consists of three events; Mogul, Stunt and Ballet, and Aerial Acrobatics. Mogul Skiing is held on a steep, heavily ridged hill with sharp drops, knife-edged bumps, and stair-stepped ruts. Competitors are judged on their speed, control, number of turns, and aerial maneuvers. Falls are frequent and heavily penalized. The Stunt and Ballet event is held on a smooth slope with a gentle gradient. Artistic continuity, difficulty of stunts, and precision of execution are weighed by the judges in scoring this event. Aerial competition can be organized several different ways. In all cases, competitors are evaluated on the difficulty of the maneuver, the height, and the distance traveled through the air.

The primary emphasis here is on the Stunt and Ballet and Aerial Acrobatic events, although the information presented in the biomechanics chapter, "The Ski Machine," can also be used to improve Mogul skiing. Beginning Freestylers may briefly skim the book, but they should definitely start with the first chapter, "Accelerate Learning Safely," to reduce exposure to injury, and to speed up the learning process. The more skillful can begin with other chapters, but time spent reading all the chapters will increase their understanding of ski and body mechanics.

Each skill or maneuver is presented with a recommended learning procedure. It is possible to skip steps or develop another learning progression, but it is highly recommended that all the beginning Freestyle maneuvers be mastered before moving ahead to the more complicated stunts.

The photographs included with each maneuver are meant to complement the written descriptions. Together they can provide a complete mechanical description of the maneuver. Sometimes the pictures may reveal a helpful point that was not mentioned in the written description.

It is even more true that a picture cannot present all of the information that is needed for complete understanding. Obviously it is impractical to show every segment of the stunt. Instead, we photographed each key part and arranged the shots sequentially. Look at the picture, read the description, and form a mental image of the actual motions involved in each maneuver before practicing. The learning steps should be mastered in sequence, each step practiced a number of times until the entire stunt can be accomplished.

Many stunts were not included—this book covers only the basics. After these are mastered, imagination, physiological abilities, and common sense are the only limitations. We stress that you should seek professional instruction as the complexity of the maneuvers increase. Many professional Freestyle camps exist, which employ some of the best professional Freestylers in the world.

John Mohan
Walt Hiltner
Seattle, Washington, 1976

1

ACCELERATE LEARNING SAFELY

Everyone hates to be called a "slow learner." Worse yet, everyone hates to be one. Many people avoid participation in acrobatic sports because of the uncomfortable feeling that develops when they think others are watching and making judgments about them during their first awkward attempts. And they also fear possible injury when trying something new.

This chapter is meant to help skiers past the initial problems encountered in mastering a new sport.

It is our purpose to speed up the learning process and minimize potential difficulties. The recommendations, procedures, and explanations that are offered have been tried and tested by us and the many skiers we have worked with over the years. Consider their value. Use them if they apply. Discard them if you find a quicker but safer way to do the same thing.

SAFETY

The safe conduct of all activities associated with Freestyle skiing is essential to its very existence. Professional Freestylers have clearly demonstrated their concern about safe management of this sport when they instituted qualifying procedures to eliminate the competitor with a "go for broke" attitude.

Safety is everyone's responsibility. Teachers must prepare students fully before attempting a stunt, explaining in detail the hazards involved in a maneuver and how to avoid them. Students should be equally aware of potentially hazardous situations and take the initiative to continually check their equipment. Some risk is inherent in any physical activity, but needless risk is foolhardy.

FEAR, COURAGE, AND CONFIDENCE

Fear is the uneasy feeling that danger is near. Fear creates involuntary tension that can interfere with a person's concentration and hinder muscular performance. Fear, however, is no disgrace. It is a normal feeling that can safeguard our lives by causing us to think seriously about our actions. The skiers taking the biggest risk are those who refuse to admit they are afraid. While everyone suffers the involuntary tension that accompanies fear, only the novice is care-

RAISING UP ON THE TOES

first step toward mastering a new Free-style skill. However, without regard for safety, courage becomes foolishness.

Skipping the fundamentals is just plain foolhardy. The Freestyler who attempts exercises for which he is unprepared subjects himself to needless danger. Professionals practice their fundamentals continually in order to prevent bad habits and develop confidence to move ahead.

Confidence is belief that a task can be accomplished. It can replace courage through repetition and practice. The strangeness first encountered when venturing ahead is replaced by a more relaxed attitude. Tenseness decreases and refinement of the new skill begins. Confidence, gained from well-learned fundamentals and a backlog of successes, provides the desire and courage to continue working on new stunts or combinations of maneuvers.

BENT KNEE SIT-UPS

less. The accomplished Freestylist avoids taking chances.

Courage is needed to overcome fear. Courage is trying when a certain amount of risk is involved, either physical or mental. It takes courage to challenge the unknown, to venture ahead. Watch someone perform his first aerial maneuver. Note the determined expression and tenseness of his body. It takes all of his courage to ski off the jump the first time. Then note the half-surprised look and feeling of relief and pleasure when he lands on his feet. Tremendous courage is sometimes required when venturing the

CONDITIONING

If you want to make the most progress and not be slowed by sprained joints or a wrenched back, general physical fitness is a prerequisite. Improve endurance by developing cardiovascular fitness—the ability of the heart and lungs to perform under continuous stress (Cooper). Select exercises that increase your pulse rate for a sustained period of time. This must be done regularly to maintain good fitness. Depending upon your circumstances, select such exercises as running, fast walking, swimming, bicycling, etc.

Participate during the off-season in those sports that are fundamentally similar to the skills used in Freestyle skiing, such as tumbling, diving, ice and roller skating, ballet, soccer, and gymnastics.

Develop an exercise program that develops strength, flexibility, and agility. Strong, well-developed muscles are added insurance for safety, helping to prevent injury to muscles, joints, and bones.

Set up a training program composed of several exercises. Each exercise should develop a certain part of the body used in skiing. Start your training program by warming up thoroughly before beginning strenuous exercise. Jogging, skipping rope, jumping jacks, etc., can be used to avoid the serious strains that can result without proper warm-up.

Some exercises we use to develop skiing muscles include:

Raising Up on the Toes: These strengthen the calf muscles while at the same time stretching the Achilles tendon if the heel is lowered below the "flat-footed" position. This reduces the chance of tearing the tendon and gives you more power to drive your skis into the turn.

Bent Knee Sit-ups: These build up the abdominal and thigh muscles that are used for a whole host of ski maneuvers where the knees are raised and the abdominal muscles come strongly into play. Do sit-ups slowly without jerking.

Side Jumpovers: This is one of the best ways to develop the propelling power in your legs important for edge control, weight transfer, and balance. Start on one side of a box and jump back and forth over it.

SIDE JUMPOVERS: WITH BOX

KNEE PRESS

Knee Press: This develops the inside and outside muscles of the thighs, which are important for protecting the knee and help to turn the skis. Sit on the floor with your feet together and in front of you. Then try to press the knees together while the hands hold them apart. Then place your hands on the outside of the knees and try to press them apart.

Leg and Ankle Raises: These develop the thigh muscles. They are important for edging, for skiing in a flexed position, and for sitting back. Sit on a counter or table with your leg hanging down with a weight of ten pounds strapped over one foot, or have someone try to hold your foot down. Attempt to extend that leg to a horizontal position. Hold for a count of five. Lower and repeat.

Weights can be used to increase strength and endurance during strenuous exercise. Weights can be purchased or made. If you decide to make your own, use a one-gallon plastic jug or sew canvas cloth together and fill with sand.

After you have finished strenuous exercising, do stretching and relaxing exercises to increase flexibility.

Some excellent stretching exercises are:

Back Stretch: Sit on the floor and roll over backwards so your hips are over

LEG AND ANKLE RAISES

BACK STRETCH

LEG STRETCH

BACK ARCH

your head and you are resting on your shoulders. Try to touch your knees on the floor next to your head. Then straighten your legs and touch your toes to the floor behind your head.

Leg Stretch: Sit on the floor with feet spread and legs straight. Bend at the waist and touch one foot. Alternate feet. Then reach straight forward and try touching your head on the floor.

Back Arch: Lie on your back with knees fully flexed and your feet right next to your hips. Place your hands on the floor beside your head. Now push up into an arch so your stomach is higher than your head, shoulders, and hips. Look to the rear with your head. Then lower yourself and repeat.

CONDITION FOR FREESTYLE SKIING

In addition to all the exercises done for general skiing, there are a few exercises that directly relate to Freestyle skiing. These include stretching and agility

STRADDLE FORWARD ROLL

ROLL-UP IN TUCK POSITION

moves that can apply to a specific maneuver, but help for all Freestyle stunts:

Straddle Forward Roll: This forward roll is started and finished in the straddle position, that is, with feet and legs spread as far as possible. Use your hands for support when initiating the roll. This stretches your neck, back, and groin muscles, and is an excellent lead-up for Snow Contact Stunts and somersaults.

Roll-Up in Tuck Position: Squat in a tight tuck position. Roll backward along your back from your hips to your shoulders.

Balance momentarily on your shoulders and the back of your head. Use your head as a lever to push you back to your feet. Beginners can use their hands to assist in rolling up. This exercise stretches the back and neck muscles and provides practice for the tuck position during somersaults.

Spot–Pirouette–Spot: Jump up in the air and turn 360 degrees trying to spot on an object in front for as long as possible during the spin. The head faces forward as the body spins underneath. Then the head snaps to catch up and focus on the

spot again. Walk through the exercise first without jumping to get the feeling of focusing and snapping the head. This is an excellent lead-up exercise for Helicopters and developing a focus point (see Glossary). You will find out which way you like to spin best and it will help orient you in maintaining a vertical axis while spinning. Then you can practice the exercise with poles to further develop your feel for the Helicopter.

Back Arch–Half Turn–Front Support: Assume a back arch position. Look down one arm. Shift all your weight to that arm as you lift the other arm and roll over so you are facing the floor. Hold yourself in the air supported by your hands and toes. Be sure to turn in the direction that you twist. This exercise assists in developing a feel for body orientation during twisting somersaults.

Cartwheel: Start in a standing position at a right angle to the direction you intend to go. Reach down to the side, placing the lead hand close to the foot. Continue the rotating action up into a spread leg handstand position and down to the other side. Your arms and legs should be extended like the spokes of a wheel and

touch the floor in corresponding order. This exercise teaches spotting for twisting somersaults.

LEAD-UP EXERCISES FOR STUNT AND BALLET MANEUVERS

The previous exercises dealt primarily with conditioning the body for the rigors of skiing. This section deals with activities that can be used to learn a specific skill or maneuver in Stunt and Ballet skiing. As you delve deeper into this chapter, you will notice much of the responsibility for your success lies with your ability to analyze your objective.

By using your imagination, you can create and develop many of the presnow lead-up activities that will accelerate the learning process of a particular stunt. Mental review and analysis are fundamental to the success of this approach (Maltz).

The ultimate purpose of these exercises is to give the muscles a chance to develop a "feel" for what is required in completing the action and maintaining balance. As muscle memory increases, the conscious involvement of the brain in achieving the skill decreases. This is

SPOT-PIROUETTE-SPOT

BACK ARCH–HALF TURN–FRONT SUPPORT

known as a conditioned reflex. The more practice, the more automatic the action becomes. Consequently, take great care to assure correct body movements since it is difficult to break a bad habit. Make sure you clearly understand what you are trying to achieve with presnow practice before training your body to act in a particular way.

The first step in developing a lead-up exercise is to clearly determine what you want to learn or improve. Then analyze the stunt so that it can be broken down into component parts. Analyze each part. Look for a specific body action that can be improved by practice and then practice the individual skills. Work toward putting them together at the speed they'll be done on the snow. Continue to analyze your practice. When in doubt about the effectiveness of your practice, review your objective again. Determine if your lead-up exercise agrees with your purpose. You will be surprised how many Freestyle maneuvers can be almost completely learned off the snow.

CARTWHEEL

DEVELOP BALANCE

The ability to remain balanced while turning, spinning, and stepping over the other ski is a key element of Freestyle skiing. There are a number of things you can do during normal daily activities that will improve this skill.

Learn to stand balanced on one foot as a start. Concentrate on the messages being sent up from the bottom of your foot. Are you standing on your whole foot? Where is the pressure greatest on the foot? On the ball of the foot, on the heel of the foot, or generally on the whole foot? Close your eyes. Now what does the foot say? Do you feel the slight adjustments that cause the pressure to waver from the heel to the ball of the foot? You should generally remain on the whole foot; a balanced position is best achieved when the whole foot is in contact with the floor. When you closed your eyes, did your hands and arms move? Were they shifting to help maintain the balanced position? Where is your raised foot located? Was it out to the side or

11

CROSSED BALANCING EXERCISE

SPINNING ON ONE LEG

under your hip? Which requires the most amount of strength to maintain? Hold the position for several minutes and your muscles will tell you that it takes less strength for the foot to be held under the hip. Drop your head on your chest while your eyes are closed. What happened to the hips? To maintain balance, they had to move slightly backward. If the simple movement of your head can cause a change in the location of the hips, imagine how stepping over or holding a ski in a different position can affect balance.

Try hopping on one foot. Hop across the floor or up stairs. Hop from side to side over an obstacle, always landing on the same foot. Switch feet. Are you better balanced on one foot? Hold one foot up and behind in a Royal Christie position and hop (see page 14). Spin and hop.

Hop upstairs backward. Use your weakest leg for a change. Hop while carrying ski poles across the back of your wrists to emphasize a quiet upper body. Ask yourself these questions:

Where am I standing on my foot when I am the most balanced?

What position is most relaxed and takes the least amount of strength for me to hold?

After hopping, where should I land on my foot to maintain the greatest degree of stability?

How can I locate the most relaxed position while holding a ski off the snow during a maneuver?

Answering these questions will result in a better understanding of the basic principles of balance and muscle efficiency as they apply to your own body.

JAVELIN POSITION

Continue to practice and experiment at home. Become aware of how your body moves. Ask questions. A good instructor will know the answers. The more you practice at home, the faster you'll learn on the hill.

HOME EXERCISES FOR STUNTS

Continue to emphasize balance and muscle efficiency when practicing the following home exercises. You should be able to interrupt almost any maneuver and still not fall over. Practice holding the positions of the various maneuvers without skis on. Soon your body becomes accustomed to the feel of the stunt and good habits begin to develop.

Basic Stunts: Practice spinning on both feet, looking and leading with your head to get the feel of 360 Spins. Hold the Javelin position. Practice the Outrigger, Royal, Shea, and other positions without skis (see Index). Put your skis on and try the positions outside. Learn the capabilities of your body.

One Ski Spins: Without skis on, practice spinning on one leg in the different positions held during a stunt. Keep the supporting leg bent and spin on the ball of the foot. You will find the pressure on your foot will vary from the ball of the foot to the whole foot. Set a focus point and keep turning your head until you see your focus point near the end of the spin. Try to practice a spin in both the high and the low Outrigger positions. Remember to keep the leg which is out to the side off the floor.

OUTRIGGER POSITION

ROYAL POSITION

SHEA POSITION

14

SHOULDER ROLL EXERCISE

Flexibility Stunts: Warm up first. Then learn the sequence of the stunts without wearing skis. Emphasize raising the leg high when doing crossover stunts. Then put on one ski and review the whole sequence again. When you have a feel for what you are doing, take off that ski and put on the other and practice. Finally put on both skis. Practice on an area that has a slight slope, because it will be easier to clear one ski off the ground.

Body–Snow Contact Stunts: All the rolls can be learned without ever touching snow. Worm Turn, Side Roll, Forward Roll, and Shoulder Roll can be done quite slowly (see Index). The Worm Turn and Side Roll require little if any lead-up exercises.

To learn the Forward Roll and Shoulder Roll, start by learning a forward roll as in tumbling without skis on. Emphasize tucking the head so it does not touch the ground. Land on the upper back. At first use your hands and arms to take the weight of your body so your head or neck does not touch. Keep your feet close to your hips when rolling so that it is easier to get up.

For the Shoulder Roll, point your feet in one direction as in a traverse across the hill, then turn your upper body and pretend to tumble downhill. Emphasize bringing the uphill hand across the front of your body, placing it and your head close to and behind the downhill foot. This will ensure the proper twisting of your body, which helps initiate the roll and the subsequent change of direction.

CHARLESTON EXERCISE

Next, try each stunt with the poles to learn the correct placement. Keep your pole straps off to avoid spraining your wrists, elbows, or shoulders. You should never land on your poles—it is painful, incorrect, and expensive to replace bent or broken poles.

After learning how to roll and where to place the poles, put on your skis. Roll up on your back and learn how to roll down by tucking your feet next to your hips while turning your skis to the side to avoid catching the tails of the skis on the grass, run, or practice area (see page 96, Completing Rolls). Then try the whole maneuver.

Some of the skills required in a Hip 360 Spin can be practiced by learning how to spin on a smooth surface such as a waxed floor. Determine where to balance on your hip so you can spin on it with your feet off the floor. Practice spinning in a circle, balanced on one hip with your feet off the floor and the upper body leaning back and in the direction of the spin to counterbalance holding the raised feet off the floor. With a little more ingenuity, many more exercises can be developed to further progress.

KIP-UP

Pole Stunts: Tip Rolls and Pole Flips can be practiced on grass without wearing skis or pole straps. In Tip Rolls, get the feeling of rolling over and looking up over your shoulder in the direction of the spin. Try it first with no poles. Start in a push-up position and push off with the hands in the direction of the spin while looking over the shoulder. Then try it with poles. Push off with both feet for

HIP 360 SPIN EXERCISE

17

TIP ROLL

spring, and bring the feet next to the hips during the spin using the poles for support.

For the next step in the progression, run, stop with both feet together, plant both poles to the side and spring into the air to start the spin. Use the poles for support and to continue the spinning action while looking hard over the inside shoulder.

The first attempts wearing skis should occur on the snow since it provides a softer surface to land on. The same goes for the Pole Flip. Practice the flipping action with a spotter on a field without skis. Put the skis on when you have a soft cushion of snow to fall upon.

LEAD-UP EXERCISES FOR AERIALS

Aerial practice requires time spent in the air. Aside from jumping off curbs, rock

POLE FLIP

walls, embankments, or other such things that provide a brief moment of "air time," most aerialists either learn by doing, or practice another activity that has closely related movements (see pages 20–25).

Air time is needed to develop a feeling for where you are in air. This is commonly called "air sense." Air sense develops with repeated practice, helping to eliminate the feeling of fear that most beginners experience. Movements become more natural and confidence develops as the body grows accustomed to the momentary feeling of hanging in air.

AERIAL AIDS

We highly recommend learning aerials by participating in a variety of off-the-snow activities. More air time can be acquired in a shorter period if a trampoline or diving board is used. Furthermore, the chance of being injured is substantially reduced because of the availability of safety apparatus.

Spotting Belts: Tumbling and twisting belts are invaluable aids in learning advanced maneuvers. Keep in mind that the purpose of the tumbling belt is not to aid the performer in gaining height or achieving correct timing, but to guard him from possible injury. Ropes should not be held taut. They should only be drawn up to reduce excess slack and to prevent them from interfering with the tumbler's movements. If a performer fails to complete a stunt or appears to be headed for a dangerous landing, the person spotting or holding the rope can control the landing by applying his weight to the rope and checking the performer's fall. Spotting belts are used the same way in tumbling and on the trampoline. Either hand-held or suspended safety belts may be used for practicing somersaults. For advanced twisting stunts, the twisting belt is indispensible, since learning in the belt is not only a safety precaution but also helps to eliminate the tenseness that occurs when approaching a new and difficult exercise.

Trampoline: The trampoline provides a dry warm place to practice, increasing the length of workouts due to increased comfort. Skill can be acquired in a shorter period because time is not wasted climbing to the top of the jump or doing other unrelated activities. It also provides some feeling of the forces involved during the landing impact. Overhead spotting belts can be used much more easily than hand-held belts. There are, of course, some disadvantages.

SPREAD

During a somersault off a jump, an aerialist must land on a slanted surface, whereas the trampoline has a flat surface for a landing area. Furthermore, aerialists do the stunts from a set position, whereas trampolinists are concerned with the rebound. In view of these disadvantages, practicing off a ski jump must not be neglected in favor of trampoline bouncing.

The Mini-Trampoline: The mini-trampoline is a small two-foot-square mat suspended by springs. Performers usually jump toward the mini-tramp, hurdle onto the mat, and spring off doing a trick, landing on a foam pad. It is commonly used at ski areas by Freestyle instructors with snow for the landing pad, so that skiers can practice most maneuvers just prior to the actual attempt off a jump. In this manner, skiers get additional concentrated practice and develop a feel for landing on a solid surface. If a slanted hill is used for a landing surface, skiers begin to develop an orientation for a balanced landing on an inclined slope.

Diving Board: The diving board is most

beneficial for Freestyle practice when the stunts are performed from a standing position on the end of the board, because the arm and leg movements of an approach and hurdle will not complicate the basic spring off the board. The diving board assists learning the spring and provides air time. However, landing in water doesn't acquaint the aerialist with the forces involved when landing on snow. Despite this disadvantage, a water landing is preferable when learning new stunts that may result in a crash.

Artificial Jumps: None of the previously mentioned apparatus enables skiers to practice the actual movements and timing of the takeoff. As most aerialists know, the takeoff (or spring) is the most critical aspect of a jump. For this reason, artificial jumps have been developed by top competitors so they can continually practice the takeoff of new maneuvers. Such practice closely simulates the actual body and ski movements that occur during real jumps on the snow. As with the trampoline and diving board, injuries that could result from serious crashes on snow are avoided due to the

cushioning effect of water or large foam rubber landing surfaces.

A Word of Caution: We have dwelled at length on apparatus that can be used in learning lead-up exercises for aerials because we have a healthy respect for the dangers involved in trying to learn them too soon without enough prior practice. If your goal is to jump and somersault, read about them carefully, get expert coaching, and start to learn the maneuvers on apparatus where you can be safely guarded and instructed. Start slowly and master each jump before moving on to the next, since each jump is different. Timing must be learned through practice, lots of practice. Remember that all of the apparatus used for teaching upright aerials and somersaults have flat, horizontal landings. Aerialists land on a steeply inclined hill that sharply drops away. Therefore, the basic body position must be adjusted from its angle at takeoff to the angle of the landing. This problem becomes especially acute with expert gymnasts or divers who have repeatedly timed their landings

for flat surfaces. A further complicating factor is introduced by the ski equipment (see Appendix), which alters the basic properties of the body and hence the rates of spin. All of this is learned by continual practice using the safest possible approach.

EQUIPMENT

The best equipment for each skier depends upon several factors, including height and weight of the skier, athletic aptitude, intended use of the equipment, durability and performance, and personal preferences. However, based upon current trends among competitors, the following guidelines should be weighed.

Skis: Stunt and Ballet skiers tend to use softer and shorter skis because they are easier to maneuver at slower speeds. The length usually varies from 135–180 centimeters. The edges are dulled six to eight inches back from the tip and tail and the center groove is filled with wax or P-tex. The lack of a center groove facilitates pivoting the skis. Certain manufacturers make a specialty ski, which is usually a

BACKSCRATCHER

little wider than the normal ski and has turned-up tails. Mogul skiers and aerialists use a longer ski for increased stability. At higher speeds in the moguls, the longer skis are much more stable, but the skis still must be short enough to fit between the moguls. Typically, lengths range from 160–200 centimeters. Aerialists use the longer skis for added stability during landing. For multiple twists, however, shorter skis are easier to maneuver, and, because they are lighter, offer some mechanical advantages (see Appendix). Selecting skis for Freestyle skiing is at best an exercise in compromise. The professionals usually have different skis for each event and short ones to practice on when attempting new maneuvers.

MULE KICK

TWISTER

Boots: There are many types and styles available. Several factors should be taken into consideration before making a purchase. Comfort is very important. Highback boots help a skier regain balance with less effort due to the higher support up the back of the leg. But how high, how stiff, and with how much built-in forward lean is a choice most skiers must make for themselves. Controversy exists concerning the amount of forward flexibility. Some want a stiff flex, which results in an immediate response in the skis when the knees are pushed forward, directing pressure to the forebody of the ski. Others like a soft flex, which allows greater flexibility in the ankle joint, making it easier to absorb moguls. Built-in forward lean helps maintain pressure on the ball of the foot, but it also forces the ankle and knee joints into a bent position, placing greater strain on the leg muscles. There are advantages and disadvantages to all styles. Body build should have some bearing on your decision. For example, if your ankle flexibility is limited and you have short, strong legs, then a stiffer boot may be best for you. However, the body is a remarkable mechanism. It seems to adjust to whatever we use or wear.

Bindings: Select top-quality bindings. Money should not be spared here. Go to a professional ski shop and get expert advice. You are looking for consistency of performance, antishock features, ease of entry and adjustment—just to start.

Poles: Poles should be lightweight and strong enough to support your body weight. The tips should be dulled to avoid the danger of harpooning yourself or someone else. Arm and shoulder injuries can be prevented by using poles with breakaway handles or no straps.

Miscellaneous Equipment: Use shatterproof sunglasses or goggles. Invest in a mouthpiece to protect your teeth during falls in hard skiing or aerials. Avoid slippery material for clothing since sliding down a mogul field on your back or side and wrapping yourself around a tree is serious. Take time to select your equipment; it is important for your performance and safety.

TERRAIN SELECTION

Selecting the best possible terrain for instruction and practice is vital for rapid progress and safety. The first thing you must consider is the other skier. Select terrain that is out of the way of heavily used traffic patterns. If you collide with another skier, it can cause severe damage, both physically and legally. Many ski areas have terrain that is especially set aside for Freestyle skiing. If your area lacks such a place, locate suitable terrain and try to negotiate an agreement with the area management.

As a general rule when selecting terrain, start with gentle, smooth slopes and work up. Steep terrain can cause all sorts of problems primarily because skiers will direct their concentration toward coping with their fear of the hill rather than the mechanics of the maneuver. Consider the following suggestions carefully and see if you can make them apply to your particular situation.

Mogul Skiing: Begin on small well-rounded moguls. The run should be short followed by a smooth runout free of trees and rocks so that a fallen skier won't slide into obstacles. Avoid heavy traffic and wet deep snow.

Work on a series of three to five short-linked turns emphasizing a quiet upper body. Learn to turn on the crest, off the side, and in the ruts between moguls. Eventually learn to ski in the fall-line linking turns together irrespective of the shape of the terrain, moving to narrower and sharper moguls to repeat the process, avoiding dangerous runouts. Learn all new actions on familiar, comfortable slopes. This builds confidence through success while the basic skills are learned.

HELICOPTER

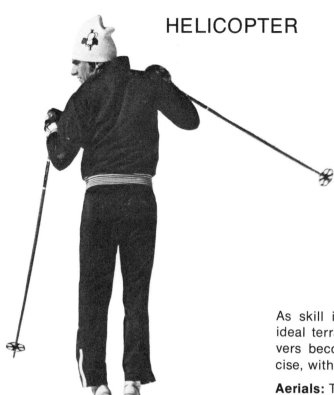

Stunt and Ballet Skiing: In Ballet competition, the slope is gentle, smooth, and well packed. Freestylists are required to perform their entire routine on the terrain selected for the specific contest. They do not have the opportunity to select a little softer snow for some stunts and bumpier spots for others.

However, when learning new maneuvers, select terrain that will promote success in the first attempts. Basic stunts should be done on a completely smooth slope, a place where no loose or unpacked snow can catch a ski and upset a person. A convex slope is best for learning 360 Spins because the tips and tails have less opportunity to catch. Pole stunts should be attempted on snow sufficiently packed to support the weight of the skier when he is pushing on his poles, yet soft enough to cushion a fall or roll. At times, a small mogul is useful for rebound to assist unweighting. Soft snow is needed for pole flips and rolls.

As skill improves, dependence on the ideal terrain decreases and the maneuvers become more automatic and precise, with fewer falls.

Aerials: The specific details of selecting terrain for aerials and jump building is covered more thoroughly in Chapter 9. However, there are a few factors that should be emphasized here. Jumps should be built on knolls with a steep landing area, out of the way of crowds. Beginners typically spend more time building and worrying over the takeoff than they do over the landing. Remember that flat landings cause severe impacts when falling from any height. Steep landings help to reduce the force of the landing impact. The inrun and outrun should be well packed and cleared of obstacles so a controlled stop can be made without interference. The lip of the jump should be hard so it will not break during the takeoff. A steep landing and long outrun that is flagged off from skiers and spectators are necessities. A spotter should be used to signal when the landing area is clear. Build the beginning jump so you are not intimidated. When in doubt, make it smaller, for it is easier to build success onto success, than success onto failure.

2

THE SKI
MACHINE

Ever since man began competing in sports, he has been looking for better ways to achieve success. Sports equipment has been constantly analyzed, evaluated, and reconstructed. Athletes have been tested, scrutinized, and subjected to concentrated forms of training and conditioning activities. Coaches are becoming experts in the many related fields that apply to the functioning of their athletes, particularly biomechanics, the study of body movement. Biomechanics includes such areas as anatomy, kinesiology, physiology, and physics. Simply stated, the biomechanics of skiing is the mechanical workings of the body, mind, and ski equipment.

Ski technicians such as Horst Abraham, Georges Joubert, Dr. Juris Vagners, and Warren Witherall are the leaders in analyzing human movement as it relates to skiing. They have studied the body to determine what movements produce the most efficient and effective results in teaching students how to ski easier, faster, and with more precision. Their constant scientific inquiry into the component parts of skiing has resulted in a wealth of printed information that

has affected the whole spectrum of skiers from beginners to world-class racers and Freestylers. They dwell on two dominant themes: a natural, balanced, ready-to-move body position, and efficiency of movement. Their purpose is to discover the best means of getting skis to do what we want them to do without unnecessary movements or an excessive expenditure of energy.

Many factors affect human balance and movement in skiing. The following summarizes a few key concepts concerning the "Ski Machine"—you and your skis. This analysis, although brief, will provide a general framework of knowledge that can be used to improve your understanding of body and ski mechanics.

BALANCE AND EFFICIENCY

Ski enthusiasts from first-day beginners to experts strive for balance and efficiency. Most recreational skiers describe this as the ability to play longer and harder with more enjoyment. They are trying to get the most out of the sport with the least amount of effort. Learning how to stand quietly relaxed on skis in a

27

ready-to-move position is a major goal of most skiers.

Competent skiing requires the body to be in a state of dynamic equilibrium, balanced in relation to all the forces acting on the body and skis. This ensures steadiness so falling is avoided. The middle ear is primarily responsible for sending messages to the brain concerning balance. However, nerve endings in the soles of the feet, in the muscles, joints, and tendons, on the skin, and in and about the muscles of the neck and head provide additional balancing information to the brain. Cold temperature reduces the effectiveness of these mechanisms, so it is important to keep the head, neck, and feet warm on cold days so that balance will not be impaired. The direct and peripheral vision of the eyes also provides visual clues as to how the body is oriented in relation to its surroundings. This network of balancing mechanisms keeps the brain informed so it can make the necessary adjustments to maintain equilibrium.

Successful balancing from side to side and/or forward to back depends upon subconscious or conscious responses to the forces that tend to upset equilibrium. These responses are usually changes in the basic body position resulting in a return to a natural position. Ideally a natural position is one in which there is a slight flexion in all the joints to maximize kinesthetic sense (body awareness) while still permitting further flexion or extension (Abraham). This ready position leaves the majority of the major muscle groups relatively free to initiate a new action or aid balancing when difficulty is experienced. This relaxed supple position allows the body to absorb uneven changes in terrain with minimum expenditure of energy.

To determine your own natural position, stand flat-footed in your ski boots. Close your eyes and seek a position where most of the muscles are relaxed. Generally your ankles and knees will be slightly flexed forward with the shins resting against the tongue of the boot due to a built-in raised heel in the boot. The upper body will be erect, the 20-pound head balanced on the neck. Your arms will be hanging to the side, but they will quickly raise to help maintain balance, if necessary. Note that some individuals may stand in a slightly different natural position, due to their unique differences in physical characteristics. Knock-knees or bowlegs will affect the way a person stands. However, no matter what the differences, understanding and using the key elements of balance will enable you to ski longer than your unknowing companions.

An integral part of balance and natural position is efficient use of muscles. Typically among beginners, excessive body motions are used to bring about the same results that the skilled athlete achieves with apparently effortless ease. The difference is that the skilled athlete has learned to make every movement count. All extraneous movements are eliminated from the performance. The task is accomplished with the minimum necessary muscle involvement, leaving the other muscles free to rest or initiate other action. Many hours of practice are necessary to achieve this state of efficiency. As skill and physical conditioning improve, the expert begins to trade off muscle efficiency for a flashy new position, or style, or sensation. This is the essence of Freestyle skiing, trading efficiency for the freedom to do what is pleasing and spectacular, while maintaining balance. Freestylers test the limits of balance and pay the price of efficiency. But it is worth it. The challenge is there, just waiting for the daring and analytical challenger.

COORDINATION

The body is an efficient organism composed of several major systems. Each system carries out a specific bodily function that is necessary for balance and performance. Without a smooth interworking relationship between all body systems, skiing would be quite difficult. The importance of rest, correct eating habits, and physical and mental conditioning cannot be overemphasized. To perform something well, your body must receive the best of treatment.

In skiing, the functions of the nervous, skeletal, and muscular systems are interrelated and have a direct effect on performance. The proprioceptors and sensory nerves perceive the unbalanced state (Logan and McKinney). The brain regulates or initiates a new action to correct the problem by sending messages to the appropriate muscle groups. The muscles contract (shorten) and pull on the adjoining bones resulting in a movement of one bone in relation to another around a joint, or stabilize one part of the skeleton against external forces. A brief review of these systems will perhaps clarify the functioning of each as it relates to skiing.

NERVOUS SYSTEM

The brain is a receiver, computer, and transmitter. Messages are sent from all parts of the body by sensory nerves to the brain. This information is received, analyzed, and interpreted in relation to the intended goal. Then a response is sent to the muscles and organs so that the task can be carried out. This system works efficiently except for a few minor problems.

Learning the correct response takes time and practice. Changing excessive body movements to specific efficient action requires repeated drill. Drill develops quicker and more automatic responses, working toward instantaneous, almost instinctive movements. Once a stunt is initiated, a skier has no time for consideration or reflection. The actions must be immediate, uninterrupted, and correct. The skier relies on learned muscle reaction. The body should have been trained so thoroughly that there is virtually no conscious thought involved; muscle action and reactions must be automatic. Thus it is important from the start to learn the correct movement. Practicing incorrect movements creates bad habits difficult to change once they have become automatic.

Emotional distress, fatigue, and unrealistic goals all impair the functioning of the nervous system. These factors interfere with the learning process. Biological changes actually take place in the body so that effective functioning is considerably reduced. The buildup of lactic acid in the muscles owing to fatigue inhibits their ability to work. Fear causes tenseness, and as a result many muscles can "chatter," blocking each other's actions as they overcompensate. Cold impairs the functioning of sensory nerves. All these factors and many more reduce the learning rate. It is imperative that attention be given to the learning environment to maximize comfort and progress. Otherwise the nervous system is working under a handicap.

SKELETAL SYSTEM

The skeleton, along with other functions, gives the body a framework, protects vital organs, and provides points of attachments for muscles. To understand how the skeletal system affects skiing, it is necessary to acquire a knowledge of what movements are possible at each joint.

The following terms describe movements that may occur at different joints in the body:

Flexion: Bending, bringing together or decreasing the angle between two bones.
Extension: Straightening or increasing the angle between two bones.
Abduction: Moving the bone away from the midline (spine) of the body.
Adduction: Moving the bone toward the midline (spine) of the body.
Rotation: Moving the bone in a circular motion around a central axis.
Circumduction: One end of a bone describes a circle while the other is

attached at a point so that the action resembles a cone shape.

Eversion and Inversion: Outward and inward movements of a bone as in the joints of the foot. (This movement is somewhat restricted by stiff ski boots; as a result this action is not of primary importance in skiing.)

The primary lower body joints that are used in skiing are the ankle, knee, and hip. The ankle is a hinge joint capable of flexion and extension only. The knee is a hinge that flexes and extends also. However, slight rotation is possible as the knee flexes to 90 degrees. Past 90 degrees of flexion, 60 to 90 degrees of rotation may be possible. The hip is a ball-and-socket joint, capable of all types of movement, restricted only by the flexibility of the muscles, ligaments, and tendons, and the surrounding bone structure. The upper body has a range of movement that is quite extensive. In the spinal column, 24 vertebrae are separated by spongelike discs, which allow a small range of movement in any direction. Although individually each vertebra can move only a small amount, collectively the sum of the small movements between each vertebra allows the spinal column to be quite flexible. Accordingly, the upper body can twist in any direction to assist turning the lower body and skis.

MUSCULAR SYSTEM

In skiing, the muscular system causes movement and resists the pull of gravity and other external forces to maintain balance and desired body alignment. Balance is maintained primarily by subconscious muscular reactions to changes in body position. These reactions were learned quite early when we were first trying to walk. As skill improved, these balancing movements became automatic so that now we rarely think about the mechanics of remaining balanced. However, once we strap skis on, we become acutely conscious of these factors. But with practice, our reactions become automatic and our next concern is how to turn our skis. Here again the muscular system has to be directed to move a body part in order to initiate or assist a turn. With practice, these muscular actions also become automatic requiring very little conscious thought.

Movement of a body part by the muscular system can be initiated in a number of ways (Vagners):

By muscles pulling against a body segment that is externally stabilized. An example of this is pushing or twisting the body by pushing against a ski that is edged in the snow.

By muscles pulling a smaller body part toward a larger body part. For example, the muscles that turn the legs are attached to the more massive hips and upper body.

By muscles pulling one body part against another body part that is already in motion. The weight or

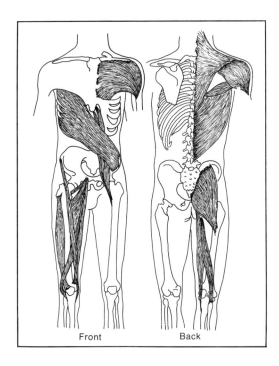

Front   Back

THE MUSCLE SYSTEM
Illustrator: Carol Rush

mass of the body part receives an additional force caused by the momentum of movement. As in rotation, once the upper body has started to twist in the direction of the turn, a set of diagonal crossing muscles of the abdomen contract to pull the legs and skis into the turn while they are unweighted. The upper body and hips provide a stable base to pull against due to their larger size and the force generated by the initial rotary movement. Thus the diagonal crossing muscles that attach to the hips, upper body, and legs pull the legs into alignment with the upper body by a strong rotary contraction.

Finally, a combination of all of the muscular actions above is used in conjunction with the ski to change direction. But remember, the body functions as a total unit and the muscular system cannot perform efficiently without a smooth interworking relationship between all body systems. The importance of maintaining a healthy physical and mental state cannot be overemphasized.

CREATING TURNS

Turns can be initiated by either a muscular action of the body or by using the ski as a tool. Ski instructors have long debated the values of different turning methods. Perhaps a brief analysis of these methods will clarify some of the advantages and disadvantages of each method. Freestylers can use them to their advantage to learn a new maneuver or improve existing stunts.

Rotation: Rotation is a quick turning of the upper body in the direction of the turn followed by a blocking of this momentum (force) at the hips, which transfers the force to the skis, causing them to turn. The turn occurs while the skis are unweighted. The rotary muscles of the legs and hips pull against the rotating upper body, causing the legs and

skis to turn and align under the upper body. This is commonly known as "blocking at the hips" or transfer of momentum. A preliminary "wind-up" before initiation provides maximum power, since the muscles are at their longest length before contraction, resulting in a strong initiation. But the wind-up position is more precarious as it increases the time necessary to do the maneuver, and it doesn't make effective use of the muscles since they are not working at their best angle of pull.

Counter-Rotation: Counter-rotation is a quick turning of the upper body opposite to the direction of the turn, resulting in an equal and opposite counteraction of the lower body, which turns the skis while they are unweighted. This is faster than rotation because there is no preliminary wind-up or transfer of momentum. The diagonal muscles of the abdomen contract, pulling the opposite sides of the upper and lower body segments toward each other while the back remains fairly erect. Because of the contorted body position created by the twisting drawing action of the upper and lower body, use of the hip rotator and leg extensor muscles is very inefficient (Abraham).

Anticipation: Anticipation is a movement of the body in the direction of the turn before the edges are released. This places the majority of the muscle groups responsible for leg rotation in their most advantageous position to work because of a bending and tilting to the side at the waist. Then, upon releasing the edges and unweighting the skis, there is a strong diagonal muscle contraction in the abdominal region that turns the legs and skis into alignment with the upper body. This is more efficient than rotation or counter-rotation because the muscles ordinarily used to prevent tipping or bending at the waist may be used to assist in turning the skis.

Leg Initiation: Leg initiation is similar to

anticipation except that there is greater involvement of the leg muscles to turn the skis while the upper body is more stabilized. This method of turning is very quick and is usually found in short-radius fall-line turns. The skis turn under the body and create the same muscle positioning and contraction as with anticipation. The upper body is stabilized, aided by a pole plant, to provide a firm base for the muscles to pull against and turn the legs. As a result, the skis turn quickly while the upper body remains relatively quiet.

The Turn Built Into Skis: The turn built into skis will occur if the skis are edged with sufficient pressure to cause reverse camber. This is due to the characteristics built into a ski such as side cut, flex pattern, torsional rigidity, and others. A ski can be bowed into reverse camber by the skier's weight or the centrifugal force generated in a turn. The ski can be placed on edge by lateral movement of the knees, hips, and/or upper body causing the ski to carve a turn in the snow according to the arc formed by the ski and its side cut. The arc of a turn can be altered by changing pressure on the ball or heel or inside and outside of the foot. Accordingly, the section of the ski having greatest pressure will cut deeper into the snow allowing the lighter section to slip out more easily. To minimize side slipping, a pure carved turn can be accomplished by equalizing the pressure or weight between the tip and tail of the ski, provided that the ski has an even flex distribution from tip to tail. The edge of the tip will cut the line in the snow, and the rest of the ski will follow the exact line with no slipping. Such a maneuver requires precise edging, reverse camber, and correct pressure distribution on the ski.

Expert skiers strive to turn their skis in the most efficient manner, making full use of the ski as a tool whenever possible since it requires very little muscular action compared to the other methods of turning mentioned above. Freestylers, however, often make such short radius turns that the skis lie almost flat on the snow so they can be pivoted under the body by muscular action.

Whether a skier uses one, several, or all the methods mentioned plus a few others to turn skis depends upon what he is trying to achieve. Racers, Freestylers, housewives, senior citizens, children, etc., all ski for different reasons. Each reason for skiing affects how and why an individual turns skis in a certain manner.

YOU AND YOUR SKIS

The ski is a tool. It was first constructed to make man's travel through snow easier. Now skis are used primarily for sporting activities. There are many different types of skis: cross country, racing, powder, recreational, freestyle, short, and others. Many skis look similar to the unknowledgeable, but each is constructed to serve a specific purpose. Each manufacturer strives to build the best possible skis that will meet the needs of the individual using them. Although manufacturers work constantly toward constructing skis that will perform the required tasks more efficiently and provide continual assistance to the skier, it is up to the skier to learn how to use the skis more effectively.

Alpine skis can be used in several different ways to make skiing easier. As previously mentioned, they can carve a turn and/or control the arc of a turn. They can assist unweighting and serve as a brake to slow down or stop. How well they do these things depends upon the characteristics built into each model, varying snow conditions, the skier's weight, athletic aptitude, and purpose. When selecting a pair of skis, all of these factors must be weighed in accordance with the manufacturer's recommendations and the suggestions of friends, instructors, and shop salesmen.

The modern ski distributes the skier's

SKI ILLUSTRATIONS

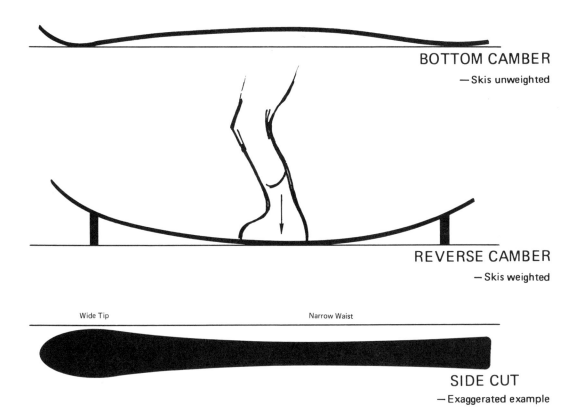

BOTTOM CAMBER
— Skis unweighted

REVERSE CAMBER
— Skis weighted

Wide Tip   Narrow Waist

SIDE CUT
— Exaggerated example

weight along its length by bowing into a reverse camber position. In soft snow this reverse camber can easily be seen. The pressure is heaviest on the ski directly under the boot and decreases as it moves toward the ends of the skis, tip and tail. As a result, the center of the ski is lowest in the snow, bowing upward toward both ends. This natural bowing of the ski can actually be used to assist unweighting if the pressure of the skier's weight is momentarily taken off the ski, allowing it to snap back to its original shape. This can be done in a number of ways. For example, by suddenly relaxing the muscles of the legs, or by actively retracting the legs, the pressure on the skis will be reduced, allowing them to snap back. Then the edges can be changed and a turn initiated during this unweighting.

Reverse camber can be increased by standing on one ski. A 160-pound weight on one ski will cause a greater bowing than the same weight distributed on both skis. Also, a turning ski or a quick edge-set (check) will increase reverse camber. Pressure on the ski increases to counteract the pull of centrifugal force generated by the turn and gravity. The increased reverse camber allows a more forceful rebound from the skis when the pressure is suddenly taken off the skis. The key to forceful unweighting is to bow the ski by increased pressure and relaxing the muscles of the legs to allow the ski to snap back to its original shape.

Skis can also serve as a brake. Slowing down is accomplished by turning the skis across the direction of travel. A check or edge-set also assists the braking process. The abrupt turning of the skis across the direction of travel is immediately felt in the legs. The strength

33

required to remain upright is drastically increased as the forward momentum tries to keep the skier moving straight ahead. The turning skis resist this action; strong legs are necessary to counteract the pull. Skiers who experience difficulty in maintaining speed control usually fail to turn their skis far enough across the direction of travel. Some of the best skiers actually turn the skis uphill before they initiate their next turn. However, most people fail to see this because of the quickness of the subsequent turn.

As mentioned before, muscular action can be emphasized to turn the skis. Turning the legs, throwing the upper body downhill, hopping the ski tips can all start a turn. But irrespective of how the skis are turned, a trained skier recognizes the ski as a tool and uses it when possible to maximize efficiency and effectiveness of movement.

THE FEET

The soles of the feet are some of the best indicators of balance. The pressure-sensitive nerve endings located in the soles can quickly tell a person when he is off balance. Too much pressure on the balls of the feet indicates excessive forward lean limiting ankle joint flexibility. Heavy pressure on the heels indicates excessive backward lean. A backward leaning position requires greater strength and somewhat restricts leg turning because many muscle groups are used to maintain this position. Standing flat-footed is the optimum balanced position, for then pressure can be exerted either forward or back by subtle movement in the ankles, knees, and hip.

Experiment by loosening your ski boots completely to explore foot feelings. Then close your eyes during a turn or while straight running. You can concentrate on the flat-footed position and the messages sent from the soles of the feet to the brain. These nerve endings can constantly keep you aware of the best position for balance. This is the next most important function of feet in skiing

besides connecting your legs to the skis.

Occasionally instructors used the words "foot swivel" as a teaching aid to get students to turn their legs. A slight rotation of the foot (inversion and eversion) is possible without turning the leg. But ski boots tend to restrict this movement so its effect is minimal.

THE ANKLE JOINT

The ankle is a hinge joint that allows the legs to be inclined 25–30 degrees forward while the foot remains flat on the floor. To reduce forward flexing at the ankle, push down harder on the ball of the foot so the lower leg begins to straighten from its flexed-bent ankle position. This action is similar to pointing the toes. By increasing pressure on the ball of the foot, the forebody of the ski will tend to remain on the snow in uneven terrain. Straightening at the ankle can also be used to vary the pressure along the length of the ski and raise the body to a higher position.

To regain balance after falling backward, the lower leg is pulled forward by the muscles surrounding the ankle joint. These muscles are weaker than the muscles that cause the toes to point. In this situation, the high back boots help since the boot supports the back of the leg by raising the fulcrum point farther up the leg. The thigh muscles pull against the supported lower leg and straighten the knee to help regain the upright position taking some of the strain off the muscles of the ankle joint.

The ankle joint also acts as a shock absorber. When a ski hits a mogul, it slows down by a slight flexing and the ankle joint begins to bend to absorb this change in the angle of the terrain. If the mogul is small, the flexibility limit of the ankle isn't reached and the ski returns to a level angle. In this case the total absorption of the mogul is in the ankle. If, however, the mogul is large, more joints must be flexed to reduce the impact of uneven terrain changes. So if a large mogul is hit, the ankle bends, then the knee, hip, spinal column, and neck, with the arms and hands moving forward to balance for the hips moving back. The ankle joint is where all the absorbing begins. Of course the stiffness and structure of the boot can severely limit this action. Built-in forward lean forces the ankle to flex to adapt to the shape of the boot. Any flexing reduces mobility and requires a greater expenditure of energy to maintain that position.

THE KNEE JOINT

The knee is a hinge joint. It flexes and extends. Slight rotation is possible with the maximum occurring after the knee is flexed 90 degrees (Rasch). Alternately bending and extending the knee helps to smooth out the ride in moguls. Ski instructors commonly use the knee as an indicator of a turning leg. Often skiers are told to push their knees in the direction of the turn to increase edging and to carve a turn. Accordingly, the knees rotate out to the side and in the direction of the intended turn, but in reality this movement is primarily a result of the swiveling action of the upper leg bone in the ball-and-socket joint of the hips.

Actually, it is difficult to discuss the actions of the knee and hip joints separately because the muscles primarily responsible for executing a turn involve both joints. Contracting the muscles to straighten the knee also causes bending at the hip. These two joint muscles play a major role in skiing, as they absorb terrain changes and make the legs turn. Consequently, the muscles of the upper leg, abdomen, and hips must be conditioned for skiing.

THE HIP JOINT

The hip joint supports the trunk (torso). It is a ball-and-socket joint, capable of movement in any direction. The muscles surrounding the hip are responsible for turning the legs and torso. Either the upper body is stabilized and the hip muscles turn the legs, or the legs are sta-

bilized, while the hip muscles turn the upper body. In either case the diagonally crossing muscles surrounding the abdomen and hips are quite strong and can initiate a variety of actions in the upper or lower body.

The center of body mass (see Appendix) is also located near the hip area. Its exact location varies according to body build and body position. The slightest movement of hips can drastically change the location of the pressure distributed on the ski. In a highly erect body position, moving the hips forward causes increased pressure on the ball of the foot. With the hips back, more weight is on the heel of the foot. Stepping from side to side causes the hip to swing over the supporting leg and tilt slightly. The location of the hips provides an excellent visual clue for analyzing balance and basic body position. The hips should be located over the supporting legs, boots, and skis for slow maneuvers, and then moved inside to counteract the centrifugal force in a turn as speed increases.

The hips provide a point of flexion close to the body's center of mass, which is also near the center of spin for all aerial maneuvers. Consequently the hips are close to the center of aerial spins. Occasionally the center of gravity can fall outside the body, such as in an open pike position when somersaulting (Batterman). However, for most practice purposes, the center of gravity in the skier's body is in the hip area.

THE UPPER BODY (TORSO OR TRUNK)

The upper body is capable of moving in any direction to varying degrees. The spinal column consists of 33 vertebrae. Of these, 24 are separated by spongelike discs that allow the individual vertebra a small amount of movement in any direction. Together they form a flexible column capable of flexing, extending, lateral flexion, and rotation.

The upper body can provide a stabilized base for the muscles that turn the legs to pull against. The upper body can be stabilized by a pole plant or turning it out of alignment with the lower body. Then a strong contraction of the abdomen and thigh muscles while the skis are unweighted results in a realignment of the hips, legs, and skis with the turned upper body. The realignment can be assisted by the action of the skis.

An action of this type is used a great deal in Freestyle skiing, particularly in 360 Spins and twisting. The upper body leads the maneuver by turning the shoulders and looking in the direction of the intended turn. The lower body follows by strong contractions of the muscles that turn the legs and by making effective use of the turning properties built into the ski.

The bending, twisting, and turning actions of the upper body also lend grace and style to the creative performance of the Freestyler as do the actions of the arms and poles. A distinctive flair can be added to intricate movements of the skis resulting in a pleasing effect that is enjoyable to watch.

THE ARMS AND POLES

The position of the arms and poles varies. For most skiers, the primary function of arms and poles is to aid balance. In previous years students were told to carry the arms and poles in a certain position. However, racing and Freestyle have done a great deal to eliminate the "positioned look."

Where should the arms be located? Let's analyze the movements of a person balancing on a rail. Where are the arms carried? Are they locked in a certain position? Most people will notice that arm position varies according to how they can be used to aid balance. A person perfectly balanced will carry his arms so one is the mirror image of the other, both arms moving up and down together. If a person is slightly off balance, then each arm will move independently of each other until balance can be obtained. Close your eyes and walk. See how the arms will aid you in keeping your bal-

ance. If you are perfectly balanced, the arms can be carried at your side. If you are unsure what to expect in terrain changes, carry the arms out to the side in a ready position where they can come to your aid more quickly.

In Freestyle skiing, the arms and poles can be used in a variety of situations. On moguls the pole can be planted lightly as a timing device to initiate a turn, or it can be slammed into the snow to push a skier back into a balanced position. It can be used to assist unweighting or turning, or to stabilize the upper body, making it easier for the leg muscles to pull against the turned upper body.

In Stunt and Ballet a pole plant can initiate a maneuver or add the finishing touches to complete it. In a 360 Tip Roll, the poles help the skier spring into the air and support his weight momentarily. In a Royal 360 the pole is used as an aid to complete the spin. The arms and poles can be used to initiate or retard motion in twists or spins. They can add force by winding up and whipping in the intended direction, transferring this motion to the body. Moving the arms away from the body will slow spinning, while bringing them in will increase the speed of the spin (see Appendix). The arms and the poles are key tools used by Freestylers to aid performance and to prevent embarrassing falls. Practice is necessary by the unskilled to determine just how hard to plant the pole. A hard pole plant can cause an off-balanced position just as easily as it can help to regain balance.

THE HEAD AND NECK

The head is for thinking. If it is cold, the functions that aid skiing do not perform well. The top of the head is responsible for a large loss of body heat when uncovered. Put on a hat before you get cold. The ears and neck should be kept warm. To combat freezing, put Vaseline on the exposed skin. Protect the eyes with goggles or sun glasses. Protect is the key word. Excessive cold or heat will impair performance or learning.

The head is balanced on the vertebrae of the neck and can pivot in any direction. The slightest movement affects the muscles of the neck, one of the major balance mechanisms in the body. Since the head is quite heavy, its movements can have a very definite effect on your center of gravity.

Experiment with head movements. Look straight ahead. Now drop your head forward. Do you feel the muscles of the neck stretch and contract? Most of you will. But did you notice the hips move backward and tilt ever so slightly? A slight movement of the head can cause a change in the center of gravity.

Have you ever heard an instructor say "Hang your head out over the downhill ski as you go through a turn"? What effect did moving the head to the side have on your center of gravity? Perhaps your instructor was trying to give you this visual-kinesthetic clue to help you get more weight on the downhill ski.

The head also contributes to motion control. Normally it can be thrown forward or back or twisted in the desired direction to initiate or check a motion. In doing so the eyes are brought into position to focus on a desired reference point or landing. This visual feedback is essential in maintaining a feel for where the body is located in reference to its surroundings.

An awareness of how to "use your head" both physically and mentally is important. Protect it and the brains inside. Use your brains and figure out more ways to learn stunts while protecting the rest of your body from damage.

Analyze the functions of your body as they relate to skiing. Many times individuals continue to practice certain activities or exercises without understanding the reasons why. You must be aware of what your body tells your mind—you may be surprised by the messages. Usually the body provides an accurate accounting of what is occurring during a specific action. A fundamental way of developing body awareness is to analyze skills and maneuvers that you can already do. Then you can concentrate on what the body says during the movement rather than trying to master a new skill.

In many cases, Freestylers are masters of body awareness. The sport evolved because many good skiers ignored the standard way of skiing. Instead they questioned and experimented, concentrating on what the soles of the feet said, what the skis did, and so on. They quickly learned the component parts of efficiency and balance. Their continuing challenge is to trade efficiency of movement in simple maneuvers for efficiency of movement in the complex gyrations they exhibit while flying down the ski slope.

The responsibility for improvement is primarily up to you. You must read, study, and analyze all aspects of body and ski mechanics to ski more efficiently. The level of skill you wish to attain will in large part determine how hard you must work to achieve your goal. You must work and study harder to ski more easily and with more efficiency.

3

BEGINNING FREESTYLE MANEUVERS

Developing the confidence to ski backwards, do a 360 Spin, and move in a variety of positions depends upon several factors. Feeling balanced and knowing how to control one's speed and direction of movement are of primary importance. Beginners make many unnecessary movements when attempting a new stunt—they appear awkward, their balance is precarious, many extra motions are used to force the completion of the stunt, and they look a little out of control. But as they practice and improve, their body movements become more refined and exactness develops. Subtleness of movement becomes characteristic as all extra actions are eliminated.

The amount of time necessary to learn a new stunt can be substantially reduced if you have a clear picture of what to do and understand why it must be done in a certain manner. Create an image of the maneuver, imagining what it looks and feels like to do it. Mental review and practice are great time-savers. Detailed analysis provides a clearer picture of the maneuver. Often, activities in other sports will relate to the new skills being attempted. Ask yourself what you are

trying to learn. Then use your imagination to see if there are any sports or activities that will assist in the learning process. An example of this is learning a diving forward roll in tumbling, an excellent lead-up exercise for Shoulder Rolls and Forward Rolls on skis.

For the most part, skiers prefer facing the direction they're traveling. Occasionally we find ourselves sliding backwards, but usually this is not by choice. We generally like to see where we are going, not where we've been. However, now that Freestyle skiing has become increasingly popular, skiers can be seen traveling down the hill in almost any position. Yet, aside from just mastering stunts, learning to ski backwards is a vital skill. It can prevent many falls and embarrassing situations. With this skill, one can confidently remain standing in many unusual situations.

Skiing backwards is a fundamental skill in Freestyle. It is an integral part of the many complex rotational tricks performed in Ballet skiing. A skilled Freestylist looks as comfortable skiing backwards as most good skiers look while moving forward. A balanced upright natural body position is characteristic of their stance, requiring less strength and allowing greater freedom of movement because the skeleton is supporting most of the body weight.

Moving backwards while running, skating, or skipping rope is good practice for emphasizing the upright position. Another key component of the stance is being able to stand flat-footed, balancing on the whole foot. Enough cannot be said about this point. Many skiers are unaware that they ski off balance because their high boots prevent them from falling over. They lunge into turns rather than using the ski as a tool.

Standing upright on the whole foot is the most efficient and balanced position in skiing. Just stand and close your eyes. Feel the subtle changes that occur along the soles of your feet to maintain balance. Feel it while balancing on just one foot. Now try hopping upstairs using both feet first. Later use only one. Some energy will be saved if a balanced upright position is emphasized. Hopping upstairs backwards is even more difficult, but it is a further refinement in developing balance. The body has to re-main over the feet. By analyzing your favorite sport or activity, perhaps you will find an exercise that can be used to develop each new skill involved in the series of stunts that follow.

BACKWARD WEDGE
(Backward Snowplow)

This is the starting point. It is a natural outgrowth of the first wedge (snowplow) you learned when you started skiing. The principles and objectives are the same. The Backward Wedge provides one of the first opportunities for speed control and emphasizes a balanced, erect, natural body position.

DESCRIPTION
Facing uphill, the tails of the skis are together and the tips apart at equal angles to the fall line forming a "V" position. Stand flat-footed with the weight equally distributed on both skis. The ankles and knees are slightly flexed. The body is upright and centered between the skis to maintain a natural balanced position. The arms are out to the side to assist balancing. The head is looking

BACKWARD WEDGE: REAR AND SIDE VIEW

downhill over either shoulder in the direction of travel. The angle of the wedge position changes according to the steepness of the slope and the speed of travel.

LEARNING STEPS

1. Select a smooth, almost flat slope for the first attempt. The slope should flatten at the bottom so you will be slowed to stop naturally. Climb just a few feet up from the flat so that speed won't be a problem. Stand with the ski tips apart, tails together, and knees to the inside so the inside edges of the skis will bite on the snow. Use the poles for support. Check your basic body position before moving. Are you standing flat-footed? Is the weight equally distributed on both skis? Are your ankles and knees slightly flexed? Is your upper body erect? Are your hands and arms out to the side to assist balancing? If this is the case, then you are ready to start.

2. Check over one shoulder to see if the path is clear. Then roll your knees out away from each other to decrease edging and push off the poles to start the

skis sliding. As you are slipping, check to see if you are still flat-footed. Slide to a natural stop or roll your knees in toward each other to increase edging causing you to stop. Make many of these runs, increasing the length and speed of the run as your confidence builds.

3. Experiment with rocking your hips forward and back to find the best balance point. Vary the angle of the wedge by pushing your feet farther apart or allowing them to run closer together. Edge one ski and release the other by moving both knees in the same direction while keeping the hips centered between the two skis. Transfer more weight to one ski and then the other. Lift one ski, then the other. Slide backwards with your feet parallel and then push them out into a Backwards Wedge to control speed. Experiment!

ERROR CORRECTION

1. Avoid bending over at the waist—it tends to put too much weight on the balls of the feet. Fear tends to make you lean forward, closer to the hill for security. Try looking over your shoulder

in the direction of travel to help maintain an upright position.

2. Beginners have a tendency to use their ski poles for support rather than concentrating on standing over their feet. Try the stunt without poles. This also helps prevent bending forward at the waist.

3. One of the hazards of experimenting is falling. When falling backwards, your knees should be bent and the head tucked to the chest so it won't be bumped. When falling to the side, try to land on your hip. You should always attempt to land on some part of the body that is large and padded. Sticking a knee or arm into the snow is dangerous because it could become stuck. If the skis split all the way out to the side in a forward fall uphill, try to land flat on your stomach, immediately bend your knees and pull the ski boots in towards your hips to free the skis from catching on the snow. When attempting new stunts at slow speeds, it is wise to set the bindings loose enough to release during a slow-twisting fall. Practice until confidence develops and success breeds the desire to move ahead. The next step is learning how to turn in this position.

BACKWARD WEDGE TURN
(Backward Snowplow Turn)

Experimenting with the Backward Wedge should have produced short radius turns caused by transferring more weight from one ski to the other. Other key factors that make the turn happen are the natural turning characteristics built into a ski, twisting the hips and upper body into an anticipated position, and turning the legs.

DESCRIPTION

Beginning in a Backward Wedge position with the weight equally distributed on both skis, a turn is initiated by transferring more weight to one ski with a sinking in the ankle and knee. This ski becomes the outside ski and steers the arc of the turn by using the natural turning characteristics built into the ski (side cut, reverse camber, flex, etc.). The hips and upper body lead the turn by twisting in the direction the ski tips are moving. The muscles of the legs pull against the twisted hips and upper body helping the legs to turn. More pressure is placed on the heel of the foot even

BACKWARD WEDGE TURN

though the whole foot remains flat-footed. When the arc of the turn is completed, rise gradually to equalize weight on both skis. The skis will seek the fall-line again. A new turn is started in the other direction by transferring more weight to the new outside ski.

LEARNING STEPS

1. In a Backward Wedge position, practice the weight transfer and looking in the direction of the turn while in a stationary position.

2. Then learn the end of the turn first. Do a slow Backward Wedge Traverse across the hill. Increase weight on the downhill ski and face in the direction of the turn. Turn uphill to stop. Keep increasing the steepness of the traverse until a turn can be started from the fall-line. Try this in both directions.

3. Link your turns together by making short radius turns down the fall-line. Start down the fall-line backwards. Transfer weight to one ski to start a turn. Before the skis have turned very far out of the fall-line, equalize the weight on both skis by rising to a Backward Wedge position. The tails of the skis will turn

back toward the fall-line. Then transfer more weight to the other ski. As skill improves turn farther and farther out of the fall-line before starting the next turn. You could set up slalom poles and practice skiing through them backwards, remembering to face away from the poles in an anticipated position.

4. Continue to experiment and ask questions. Stand on your whole foot, but change the pressure back and forth from the heel to the ball of the foot. Where is the pressure in a Regular Wedge Turn? Where is it in a Backward Wedge Turn? Just a slight change of pressure to a different spot on the foot can spell the difference between success and failure. Put your hands on your knees to emphasize the action of both knees moving toward the inside of the turn.

5. Practice on a convex or slightly rounded slope so the tails of the skis won't catch. See if the tails of the skis can be turned far enough out of the fall-line so the ski tips end up pointing straight downhill. Then shift your weight to the balls of your feet by flexing your ankles and knees and moving your hips toward the tip of the ski. A new skill has

WEDGE 360

been learned. Now it is possible to start backwards and end up going forwards.

ERROR CORRECTION

1. Beginners commonly lean to the inside, uphill, and bend at the waist when first attempting this stunt. The problem can usually be eliminated by keeping your head over the outside ski and boot. This also helps to keep your weight over the outside ski.

2. Sometimes the inside ski catches on the snow because the inside edge is still biting in the snow. Make sure both knees move toward the inside of the turn while your body remains centered between the two skis. The result is an increase of edging for the weighted outside ski so it can cut a turn in the snow while the edging for the inside ski decreases.

3. Don't push with your poles to help the turn. A push can be used to an advantage later, but at this point it is better to emphasize correct body position rather than pole plant. Ski without the ski poles during the initial stage to create a greater awareness of balance and a more upright position.

WEDGE 360
(360 Snowplow)

Now that you are starting to spin all the way around, there are a few facts to re-member. Everyone spins more comfortably to one side than the other. Experimenting will quickly tell you what side you spin to best. When first learning spins, always start by turning uphill because it is safer, easier, and you don't fall as far.

DESCRIPTION

Beginning in a Wedge position facing downhill, slide fast enough downhill to turn the ski tips completely uphill so they end up being farther up the hill than the tails. As soon as the ski tips are higher uphill than the tails, the ski tips are pushed apart into a Backward Wedge position. Then a Backward Wedge Turn is done from this position, with enough speed so the tails of the skis can be turned higher uphill than the ski tips. Then the tails are pushed apart into another Wedge position to complete the maneuver.

Throughout the Wedge 360 the angle of the Wedge position will vary. It will become narrower to gain speed and to facilitate pushing the skis back and forth from a forward to backward Wedge. The Wedge will become wider to decrease speed and to help initiate a change of direction.

LEARNING STEPS

1. Review the Backward Wedge Turn.

Practice pushing the ski tips apart and then allow them to run together under the hips. Then ski backwards down the hill with the skis in a wide track parallel position. Push the ski tips out and do a Backward Wedge Turn. Complete the maneuver with the end of a Wedge 360.

2. Now do a Forward Wedge Turn with more than the usual speed. Turn while reducing the angle of the Wedge until the ski tips are higher uphill than the tails. Then push the ski tips out and stop in a Backward Wedge position. This helps teach balance and proper upper body position over the hips and ski boots. Then finish with a Backward Wedge Turn.

3. Finally put the whole maneuver together. Pay particular attention to pressure changes on the soles of the feet noting how the pressure shifts along the sole several times during this maneuver.

ERROR CORRECTION

1. Failure most frequently occurs during the change from forward to backward turning. Bending forward at the waist, leaning off balance, or forgetting to look in the direction of the intended turn are the common errors. Balance is critical. Remain over both skis, upright, and look back in the direction of the new turn as the pressure shifts to the heel of your foot.

COMPLETING SPINS:
SHORT RADIUS

2. Try to increase your speed so you will begin skidding as in a Christie Turn. If you decrease the angle of the Wedge, it will develop eventually into a Parallel 360.

COMPLETING SHORT RADIUS 360 SPINS

Mastery of completing Short Radius 360 Spins is a key step to all rotational 360 Spins. The basic body movements and positions required apply to the majority of the 360 Spins done on either one or both skis. The 360 Spin maneuver is one of the hardest skills for beginning students to learn, but it opens the door to a multitude of other ballet maneuvers.

The most commonly used method of completing a 360 is spinning in a short radius. To accomplish this maneuver, more pressure is applied to the front of the skis as they sit almost flat on the snow during the last half of the spin. As a result, the ski tips will seek the fall line.

DESCRIPTION

1. Decrease the edging of the skis so they sit almost flat on the snow by rolling the knees in the direction of the spin.
2. Apply more pressure to the front of

the skis by standing heavy on the balls of the feet.
3. Anticipate or lead the spinning skis with the upper body by turning the hips, torso, and arms, and looking in the direction of the intended spin.
4. Plant the outside/uphill pole to assist forcing the skis through the turn and to emphasize leading the spin with the upper body. However, one disadvantage of an "assisting pole plant" is that it creates a dependence on the pole for balance and initiation. It also involves the use of many more muscles and somewhat restricts freedom of movement.

LEARNING STEPS
1. A brief review of the running exercise while continually spinning and turning from a backward to forward position will provide some physical training that is similar to the actual performance on the snow. This exercise stresses a tall upright position, looking in the direction of the turn, and keeping the feet generally right under the hips.
2. Once on the snow, a variety of exercises can be used to develop the slipping, spinning action while moving backwards. Face across a steep hill and spread your poles out to each side. Using the poles for support, try to get the ski tips to slip downhill from the uphill pole

COMPLETING SPINS: LONG RADIUS

to the downhill pole. Roll your knees downhill to decrease the edging and initiate the slipping. Push your knees back into the hill to stop the slipping. Then try a short slip without pole support, trying to keep your hips right over your feet in a balanced position.

3. Do a Backward Wedge across the hill, lift the uphill ski and bring it in parallel to the slipping downhill ski. Continue to slip backwards on both skis in a parallel position trying to get the ski tips to slip down toward the fall-line. Start a Backward Wedge, turn from the fall-line, and bring your inside ski parallel earlier each time. Use a small mogul to help initiate the slipping. Slip backwards while your skis are slightly edged and gradually decrease edging. Vary the pressure from the balls of your feet to the heels. Analyze how these factors affect the action of the skis.

4. Sideslip forward and then back, attempting to make the ski tips climb uphill and then dropping toward the fall-line. Do an Uphill Christie on a steep hill to stop. Then slide backwards trying to get the tips to drop. Keep increasing the angle of the backward slipping until the slipping starts when the ski tips are facing straight up the fall-line. Once this has been mastered, you know the end phase of many of the ballet tricks that follow.

COMPLETING LONG RADIUS 360 SPINS

Another method of completing a 360 Spin is to turn with more pressure on the tail of an edged ski letting the ski tip skid through the turn. This method is seldom used because it is more difficult to remain balanced while leaning back. In addition, more leg strength is required to hold the body upright and the turning movements of the legs are more restricted since many muscles are used to maintain this position.

DESCRIPTION

1. More pressure is exerted on the tails of the skis by rocking the hips backwards, putting more weight on the heels of the feet.

2. The upper body is pivoted in the direction of the spin as the hips drop back and inside.

3. The skis are pulled through the turn by contracting the muscles of the legs to pull against the anticipated hips and upper body.

4. The skier leans to the inside so the tails of the skis carve on the snow because of increased edging.

5. Upon completion of the spin, the skier rises to a balanced position, standing flat-footed.

PARALLEL 360 SPIN

LEARNING STEPS

1. Usually this maneuver is first attempted in a Backward Wide Track parallel position. Begin by traversing across the hill backwards, then lean back and inside to pull the skis into the turn. Remember to pivot your hips and upper body in the direction of intended turn to anticipate the turn.

2. Increase the beginning angle until a long radius turn can be done starting straight down the fall-line. Sometimes it is necessary to unweight the skis to start the turn, in which case a quick dropping of your hips will result in momentary unweighting to break the skis loose. Another way is to lean backwards and hop the tips of the skis downhill while moving.

As the skill level increases in completing 360 Spins, more difficult exercises can be used to develop a keen awareness of balance. Try the above exercises with your eyes closed to improve awareness of pressure distribution on your feet. Another variation is to hold your arms tight against your body so that the arms and hands cannot be used to aid balance. Practice knee-rolling exercises to improve edge control. All of these exercises will develop an awareness of standing with your hips directly over your feet and should be practiced in as many different ways and conditions as possible. Such practice will provide invaluable preparation for the complex stunts to follow.

PARALLEL 360 SPIN

An integral part of this stunt has already been explained, in Completing Short Radius 360 Spins. Once that skill has been mastered, the tricky part of the Parallel 360 Spin maneuver occurs just as the edges are changed from a typical Uphill Christie to a flattened unedged ski with slightly more pressure on the balls of the feet. The secret is to turn at least to the point where the ski tips face straight uphill before flattening the skis.

DESCRIPTION

From the fall-line, an Uphill Turn is carved by driving the ankles and knees forward and to the inside of the turn. This action causes the edges to bite in the snow and increases pressure on the front of the skis. The tails of the skis will slide out. The turn is carved until the skis are pointed straight up the hill or a little beyond. Then edging is decreased by moving the knees directly over the skis.

BALANCING ON ONE SKI: UPRIGHT AND TO THE SIDE

To complete the 360 Spin, slight forward pressure is maintained on the unedged skis with the body maintaining an anticipated position leading the spinning skis. Leg turning and pushing with an outside/uphill pole plant can be used to assist the spin. As the spin is completed, rise gradually to a flat-footed stance evenly balanced on both skis.

LEARNING STEPS

1. Practice the end of the turn first. Review the mechanical movements involved in Completing Short Radius 360 Spins and Uphill Turns before putting the two together. Remember to continually turn your head in the direction of the spin, looking ahead to see where you are going.

2. Try it first in a Wide Track stance. If difficulty occurs, you can always push the skis out into a Wedge 360. As balance improves, start bringing your feet closer together.

3. As skill and continuity increase, experiment with different terrain. Start your turn on the front side of a mogul. Do one-half to two-thirds of the turn before reaching the crest, and pivot your skis the rest of the way around while sliding off the backside of the mogul. Do a Parallel 360 on banks and sidehills. This stunt can be performed safely in many spots, adding a little spice to those long, smooth intermediate runs.

ERROR CORRECTION

1. Avoid banking or leaning to the inside when doing the Uphill Turn by keeping your ski boots directly under your hips. A slight leaning will occur naturally to counteract centrifugal force, but don't exaggerate it.

2. Over-edging and leaning to the inside can be substantially reduced by practicing sideslipping exercises. Emphasize lateral knee movement with very little change in body position.

3. Emphasize looking over the shoulder to assist anticipation and standing erect. Select a spot or focus point at the end of the spin and keep turning your head until you see it. The focus point will remind you to lead the spinning skis with your upper body and head.

BALANCING ON ONE SKI

Standing, traversing, or turning on one ski in a balanced position requires an understanding of efficient muscle and skeletal usage. When the bones of the skele-

ton are balanced, one on top of another, the majority of body weight is carried by the skeletal structure. This arrangement frees many muscles from a supporting function they must perform when the bones are not lined up, resulting in a reduction of the amount of energy expended.

Standing upright while holding one raised ski and boot under the hips is a very efficient balanced position. The head is balanced on the spinal column, which is supported by the hips. One leg supports this total weight. Naturally this leg tires quickly since it is doing the job normally done by both legs.

Raising the leg to the side requires more strength. The smaller muscles along the outside of the leg must hold it in position. In addition, the upper body has to lean to the opposite side in order to counterbalance the raised leg. Many muscles along one side of the body are used to hold this position. The head is no longer supported by the skeleton so that the muscles of the neck, chest, shoulder, and back are now working to keep the head erect. If you are thrown off balance in this position, your body must be straightened and realigned before it can react to the difficulty. The muscles

responsible for maintaining an unusual position must, therefore, be freed from their supporting role in order to function as needed to regain a balanced position.

Freestylists study each new position in order to determine how balance can be achieved. They realize that whenever they move one part of their body to a different position, something else must be adjusted to counterbalance the new position. This is where the tradeoffs begin. Efficient balance and muscle usage are traded off for new and unusual positions requiring a great deal of strength in a precarious position.

JAVELIN TURN

A Javelin Turn is an excellent beginning stunt because it is done with all of the weight on the outside ski, as are the majority of turns taught in regular ski school classes. Once you understand the principles of efficient balancing on one foot and can do a skidding turn, you are ready to make a first attempt.

DESCRIPTION
A Javelin Turn is done on the outside ski. Immediately after a regular Christie Turn is initiated, the inside ski is lifted com-

JAVELIN TURN

pletely off the snow and crossed over the outside ski just ahead of the boot. Both boots are close together. The raised ski points to the outside of the turn. When the turn is completed, the inside ski is uncrossed and lowered to the snow.

LEARNING STEPS

1. First practice the Javelin position standing still. Notice the raised boot is located just above and close to the other boot. Close your eyes to get the feeling of a balanced position. Concentrate on the messages being sent from your foot to your brain. Often it is helpful to close your eyes for a brief instant during a turn to determine if you are standing on the whole foot. Practice traversing on your downhill ski in this position.

2. Begin to assume this position at the end phase of any skidded turn. Initiate a Wedge Christie, an Uphill Christie or a Parallel Turn. After these turns are three-fourths completed and the skis are still skidding, shift all your weight to the outside ski. Lift the inside ski and cross it over in front of the outside ski.

3. As your balance improves, work backwards through the turns trying to assume the Javelin position earlier each time. Eventually a turn can be started from the Javelin position and held as the skis pass through the fall-line.

ERROR CORRECTION

1. Leaning to the inside of the turn makes it difficult to remain balanced. Leaning inside is usually caused by pushing hard on the outside ski and stiffening the ankle and knee. To correct the problem, emphasize settling onto the weighted ski and let the front of the boot support the ankle. Your head should remain over the outside ski.

2. The raised ski sometimes throws a beginner off balance. Loss of balance is a result of failing to keep the raised ski boot right next to and over the other boot. Try closing your eyes during a turn. Usually, the loss of visual input will

graphically communicate where you are standing on your foot.

TURN ON THE INSIDE SKI

Time spent balancing and hopping on one foot across lawns and up stairways will pay off in learning this turn. Turning on the inside ski is a basic skill that bridges the gap between the basic stunts already covered and the single ski stunts that follow.

Normally, it is more difficult for most people to turn on the inside ski due to the requirements that must be met in order to achieve a balanced position. If a skier is balanced on the inside ski, he doesn't have another inside ski to fall back on if difficulty is encountered, and the only recourse is to hop to regain balance or fall. Leaning to the inside (banking) is very common in this turn because it helps to counteract centrifugal force. Determining the degree of lean while achieving efficient muscle usage is a major problem.

DESCRIPTION

Beginning in a traverse crossing the hill, the downhill/inside ski is lifted off the snow and stepped toward the fall-line with a push off the uphill/outside ski. This is similar to a skating step. The upper body moves downhill over the inside ski to retain balance. The outside ski is held off the snow and trails behind the inside ski. Control of the turn is accomplished by subtle forward pressure on the ball of the foot and lateral knee movements to control edging. As the arc of the turn is completed, rise gradually, bringing the outside ski down, decrease the pressure on the ball of the foot, and resume a new traverse.

LEARNING STEPS

1. To begin learning this turn, stand on both skis with your arms held out to the side for balance. Lift your downhill ski off the snow, holding the downhill boot under your hip. Search for a comfortable upright position. Memorize the feeling of

TURN ON THE
INSIDE SKI

this position, paying particular attention to the flat-footed feeling from the sole of your foot.

2. Start across the hill in a slow traverse standing on both skis, and gradually transfer more weight to the uphill ski by moving your hips and head over the uphill ski. Begin raising the downhill ski off the snow by lifting the downhill boot up under your hip. Practice holding the downhill ski in different positions making sure the raised boot remains close to or under your hip.

3. While standing still, drive your knee forward and uphill toward the inside of the turn. This action is similar to the motion required to carve a Turn on the Inside Ski. Keep the outside ski off the snow while practicing. Shift from a flat-footed position to one with more pressure on the ball of your foot as your knee moves to the inside of the turn. Then return to the flat-footed position.

4. From a traverse, initiate an Uphill

OUTRIGGER POSITIONS: HIGH AND LOW

Turn while standing on both skis. Halfway through the turn, shift your weight to the inside ski and lift the outside ski, completing the turn on one ski. Pick a steeper traverse and try to step sooner into the inside ski. Work on stepping from one ski to the other.

5. Practice skating steps on the flat or a very gentle hill. Aim down the fall-line on a gentle hill and skate onto the inside ski. Before doing a complete turn, stand still and practice lifting the downhill/inside ski, then stepping toward the fall-line with a push off the uphill/outside ski. Now try it moving. Speed will help the learning process. As your skill increases, try to keep the raised boot near or under your hip to decrease the amount of inward lean.

ERROR CORRECTION

1. If you experience difficulty with balance, you can practice sideslipping on the uphill ski. As your confidence increases, slip more down the fall-line, trying to make the tips turn uphill with increased forward pressure. The head and upper body should remain over the skis during this exercise.

2. Avoid leaning too far forward or bending at the waist. While it is possible to do a turn this way, a bad habit may be created that is hard to break when learning 360 Spins. Emphasize an upright position.

3. Stiff ankles and knees reduce edge control. Settle into your boots and concentrate on a relaxed flat-footed stance from which subtle changes of pressure can be exerted.

OUTRIGGER TURN

The Outrigger is a low, balanced position that is used as a link between tricks or as a recovery maneuver when balance is lost in Ballet or Mogul skiing. The Outrigger appears to be performed with weight on both skis, but looks are deceiving. Really it is just a turn done on the inside ski in a low position. The outside ski is just dragging or sliding on the snow supporting very little weight, if any at all.

The Outrigger position places a great amount of stress on the support knee. If an individual has a history of knee trouble or cannot comfortably remain in the low Outrigger position, avoid this maneuver altogether. The only other alternative is to do the Outrigger in the high position. In this case the knee is flexed no more than 90 degrees with the thigh approximately parallel to the snow. One final comment about knees—keep the extended leg slightly flexed at the knee to prevent locking of the knee joint and thus reduce the chances of injuries

caused by the ski catching on the snow.

DESCRIPTION

In the Outrigger position the weight is primarily on the uphill ski. The uphill knee and hip are fully flexed with the downhill leg extended to the side and the boot dragging on the snow. The chest is centered over the uphill knee and the arms are held out and forward for balance. The weight should be distributed evenly on the sole of the uphill foot. (The built-in forward lean and flex of the ski boots may sometimes prevent even weight distribution.)

An Outrigger Turn is initiated in the same manner as a turn on the inside ski. Starting in a traverse, the downhill/inside ski is lifted. The edges are changed as the skier pushes off the uphill/outside ski, stepping toward the fall-line with the inside ski in a skating motion. The upper body is lowered with the hips and head remaining over the inside ski. The hands are held forward and out to the side to help maintain balance. The outside leg remains extended to the side with knee slightly bent. The outside boot and ski drag along the snow in such a manner as to prevent catching on the snow and pulling the skier off balance. The arc of the turn is completed on the inside ski with subtle pressure forward on the ball of the foot and increased edging.

Linked Outrigger Turns require remaining in a squatted position between turns. At the end of an Outrigger Turn, the extended leg is brought in under the hips so both skis are parallel in the squatted position. The skis are weighted equally with more pressure on the ball of the foot. The knees begin rolling downhill to flatten the skis on the snow, causing them to seek the fall-line. Then, by pushing off the outside ski in a squat skating motion, a new Outrigger Turn is initiated.

LEARNING STEPS

1. First practice the Outrigger position while stationary. Remember, if your knees hurt or the position causes strain, evaluate the possible consequences. Either avoid the Outrigger or do it in the high body position.

2. Practice an Outrigger traverse, extending the outside leg downhill. Be sure to select terrain that is packed smooth to avoid catching the extended boot and ski on loose snow. There should be no body movements required to maintain this position and the only adjustments should be for changes in terrain.

3. Work into Uphill Christies, lowering into the Outrigger position during the turn. Practice the skating step before initiating a turn and crossing through the

LINKED OUTRIGGER TURN

fall-line. Then initiate a turn on the inside ski and immediately lower yourself into the Outrigger position.

4. When learning to link Outrigger Turns together, practice first without skis. Assume an Outrigger position. Bring the extended leg under the hips into a squatted position, then extend the other. At first the movements can be done in a fairly high squat. As smoothness develops and your balance increases, your position can be lowered gradually until the stunt is done in the lowest possible position.

5. Once on the snow, start in the squatted position facing down the fall-line. Push one ski to the side to help get your weight over the other ski and initiate the turn. Then try a traverse lowering to a squatted position. The knees should roll downhill over the skis to reduce edging. If the weight is forward and the skis are flat on the snow, the tips will seek the fall-line. Finally, put the whole maneuver together.

ERROR CORRECTION

1. The most common error is catching the inside edges resulting in a "belly flop" on the snow. To eliminate this problem, the uphill knee pushes uphill while your head remains over the uphill ski. The position of your head acts as a reminder to keep your hips over the uphill ski.

2. Occasionally the extended ski will catch on the snow and pull a person off balance. Remember to keep the weight off this ski. It should be extended to the side, not allowing it to fall behind where it can catch when the ski begins to turn

to the side. The extended ski should be pointing in the same direction as the weighted ski.

ROYAL CHRISTIE

The Royal Christie is a widely recognized maneuver. It can be done in a high or low

position. The upper body can either be bent forward at the waist in a position parallel to the snow or held fairly erect. In both cases, the back is arched.

The high position is considered quite beautiful. In this position it is easier to change quickly to another position since the body is already upright, but considerable strength is required to hold the raised ski off the snow. In the low position, bending forward at the waist acts as a counterbalance and helps to offset the weight of the raised ski reducing the amount of strength needed to hold the position. Selecting what style to use depends upon an individual's strength, flexibility, and the stunt that will follow the Royal Christie.

DESCRIPTION

A Royal Christie is initiated in the same manner as a turn on the inside ski. With a push off the uphill ski, the downhill/inside ski is stepped in the direction of the turn onto a new edge. The outside/uphill ski is raised up and behind the hips by bending the knee with the ski tip pointing to the rear with the arms held out and forward to aid balance. The turn is continued by driving the ankle and knee in the direction of the turn. The resulting increase in edging and pressure on the front of the ski causes the edge to carve in the snow while the tail slips out. As the turn is completed, there is a gradual rising, decreasing pressure on the front of the ski and a lowering of the raised ski to the snow.

LEARNING STEPS

1. The Royal Christie position should be practiced while standing stationary. Experiment with the location of the raised trailing boot. Notice that leaving the boot out to the downhill side causes you to lean to the uphill in order to compensate and remain balanced. Pushing the raised boot completely behind your hips and to the uphill side causes your upper body to lean downhill. Understanding the way in which the position of the raised boot affects the location of the upper body will aid in linking different stunts with the Royal Christie. Preferably, align the raised boot directly be-

ROYAL CHRISTIE TURN

ROYAL CHRISTIE POSITIONS

CHARLESTON

hind your hips when doing just one turn.

2. After the Royal has been practiced in a stationary position, try it moving in a very slow traverse, concentrating on remaining flat-footed. Skate into a Royal traverse by pushing away the tip of the downhill ski in a skating motion allowing it to swing up and behind into the Royal position. As your balance improves, increase your speed and drive the ankle and knee forward and inside to start a small turn up the hill. Keep increasing the speed and aim more into the fall-line. Work toward doing an Uphill Christie in the Royal position.

3. Do a complete turn on the inside ski, lifting the outside ski into the Royal position near the end of the turn. Keep lifting the outside ski, working backwards through the turn. Start a traverse and skate into the fall-line. Push the outside/uphill ski tip away from the inside ski. Continue pushing the tip back and raise it off the snow into a Royal position. Now you have done a complete Royal Christie.

4. Experts usually link Royals together with a slight hop. The hop is used to unweight the skis so the edges can be changed when starting in a Royal posi-

tion. Many times it is difficult to see the hop—the better the performer, the harder it is to detect the hop.

ERROR CORRECTION

1. Most difficulties in the Royal are due to improper balance. Don't lean too far forward or bend excessively at the waist. Be careful not to stiffen your ankles, locking them into a position so they are unable to flex and extend naturally to absorb the unevenness of the terrain. If you allow the raised ski boot to swing to the outside of the turn away from your hips, it will pull you off balance. You must remain close to the center of the turning ski using your arms to help balance.

2. If you have difficulty lifting the raised ski off the snow, usually this is caused by a failure to bend the raised knee. Sometimes it is a lack of strength, dictating that the low position must be used.

CHARLESTON

The Charleston requires rapid changing from ski to ski in a hopping motion. Consequently, it is an excellent lead-up maneuver for Legbreakers, Downhill Crossovers, or any other maneuver that requires rapid weight transfer.

DESCRIPTION

The Charleston consists of linking short radius turns on the inside ski down the fall-line in a rhythmical manner, accompanied by an edge-set and pole plant. The new skill that must be learned in this maneuver is hopping or stepping from one inside ski to the other while maintaining speed control. The pole is planted to signal the unweighting and switching of skis on the snow.

LEARNING STEPS

1. Start practicing this maneuver while standing stationary on flat terrain. Lift one ski off the snow and then hop off the other ski. Put the first ski down in the identical spot that the second ski just left. By hopping from one ski to the other with both skis continually landing in the same spot, the raised ski will naturally be moved out to the side to make way for the landing ski. This action creates a swinging movement of the skis under the body.

2. Draw a single line on the snow between your skis. Try to hop over the line so the landing ski lands farther under your body. Then repeat with the other ski. For example, hop the right ski

over the center line landing under the left hip. The left ski will swing farther out to the left side to get out of the way. Then hop the right ski. Swing it to the right while the left foot swings under the right hip. Land on the inside edge of the left ski. Repeat.

3. Practice this down the fall-line starting with a long radius turn on the inside ski. Set an edge and plant your pole. Swing the skis under the hips landing on the inside edge of the opposite ski. Repeat the process. Keep reducing the radius of the turn.

ERROR CORRECTION

1. It is difficult for some people to establish a rhythm because of the strength and agility required to perform this stunt. Hopping from leg to leg wearing heavy ski equipment is tiring. Try skipping rope at home to develop rhythm. Singing a rhythmical tune also helps to establish a beat. Concentrate on swinging the skis to the rhythm of the tune.

2. Having the weight back is another common error. Maintain sufficient ankle and knee flex to remain balanced while absorbing the landing impact, edge-set, and swing of the skis. Those having difficulty with landing in a balanced position can practice this exercise at home by skipping rope.

3. Sometimes it is difficult to get the ski out of the way when the other one is swinging under for the landing. This can be avoided by bending the knee sharply, lifting the ski off the snow and away.

These are the basic Freestyle maneuvers. They provide the foundation skills for the many stunts to follow. Many times you may refer back to the text to clarify your understanding of some of the beginning stunts and their relation to the complex maneuvers to follow. Keep working, for the fun has just begun.

4
ONE SKI SPINS

The maneuvers described here are by no means the most difficult and complicated of all the varied stunts developed and performed by Freestylers. They are, however, sufficiently difficult to place them in a group more advanced than the basic maneuvers.

The problems faced by Freestylers in performing these more advanced stunts are neither new nor strange. The basic requirements of balance, edge control, and efficiency of movement still exist. But as the maneuvers increase in complexity, meeting these requirements becomes more difficult. The action becomes faster and more complicated. More skills must be coordinated with greater precision. But here, as always, thorough training in the fundamentals coupled with determination and courage will enable you to meet and master each succeeding maneuver.

Learning One Ski Spins can be facilitated with dry-land practice. Just spinning on one leg, holding the other leg in the various positions typifying certain stunts, will greatly improve balance and muscular feel. Concentrate on looking in the direction of the turn and twisting your upper body in an anticipated position ahead of the turning foot.

Learning new spins can be accomplished more easily and safely on the snow by turning uphill at first toward your good side. By trying all maneuvers both ways, you can find out which side is more comfortable for you. Learn the trick to your good side first. As confidence develops, switch feet and try it the other way. All the spins can be done up or down the hill and on either foot. An expert Freestyler should be able to spin in all the various directions using either ski.

FINISHING A ONE SKI SPIN

The directions for finishing a One Ski Spin are identical to the directions for Completing Spins (page 46) except that one ski is held off the snow. Skiers find this spin more difficult because greater precision is required to maintain balance and complete the stunt. The key factors are the same; however, now they must be done with more precision to achieve success. It was possible in previous 360 Spins to de-emphasize some key elements and still make it around. This

TIP DRAG 360

won't be the case now. One must strive toward perfection in each component part to achieve the end result.

DESCRIPTION

During the last half of a 360 Spin, the outside ski is lifted off the snow while the raised boot is held under the hip. Forward pressure toward the tip of the ski is maintained by standing more heavily on the ball of the foot. The knee is rolled directly over the ski to decrease edging and allow the ski to slip. The head and upper body twist in the direction of the turn to anticipate, allowing the leg muscles to pull against the anticipated upper body to help turn the leg and ski. The outside pole can be planted to assist the turning of the body and skis. The spin is completed by rising, equalizing pressure over the whole foot and lowering the raised ski to the snow.

LEARNING STEPS

1. Do a closed stance 360 on both skis. Lift the outside ski off the snow just as the maneuver is nearing completion.
2. Continue lifting the outside ski earlier in each attempt, swinging the raised foot in the direction of the spin to provide a little momentum that will assist the completion of the turn.

ERROR CORRECTION

1. If you lean to the inside during the initial phase of a 360 Spin, it will be extremely difficult to remain balanced over one ski when the ski is flattened on the snow. Emphasize keeping the upper body centered over the turning ski.
2. Avoid becoming square over the ski during the spin. Keep leading the turn with the upper body so your leg muscles can pull against the twisted upper body.

TIP DRAG 360

The Tip Drag 360 is an excellent lead-up stunt for a One Ski 360 Spin. It develops a feeling for anticipation and keeping the hips centered over the turning ski. The Tip Drag 360 can also be combined with a Backward Royal Christie to make a beautiful stunt.

DESCRIPTION

The inside ski is lifted off the snow and the leg turned so the ski tip points to the inside of the turn. The ski tip is lowered and allowed to catch or drag on the snow. The dragging tip slows the forward progress of the inside leg, hip, shoulder, and arm, causing the body to pivot in the direction of the spin leading the turning ski in an anticipated position. The skier spins uphill 180 degrees on one ski. Then both skis are brought together and are equally weighted. The spin is completed with forward pressure on flattened skis. A pole can be planted to assist in the completion of the spin.

LEARNING STEPS

1. While standing still, practice raising the inside/uphill ski off the snow,

ONE SKI 360 SPIN

bending the knee and keeping the ski boot near your hips. Swing the tip of the raised ski back and to the side in a circular motion putting the ski tip on the snow. The angle between both skis should resemble a pie shape similar to a Backward Wedge position.

2. In a slow traverse, lift the inside/uphill ski and "catch" the tip of the raised ski on the snow causing the body to begin facing uphill in the direction of the intended spin. Keep the raised ski boot as close to or under your hips as possible to maintain a sturdy balanced position while spinning 180 degrees. Then set down the raised ski parallel to the other and complete the 360 Spin on both skis.

3. As your skill increases, try completing the last 180 degrees of spin on one ski with the other ski raised off the snow. This action will assist the upper body in facing the direction of the turn and provide a beautiful ending for a Tip Drag 360.

ERROR CORRECTION

1. Difficulty in catching or dragging the tip is usually caused by raising the ski too far off the snow so it is almost impossible to hook the edge of the ski tip. Another cause of this problem is failing to turn the leg as it raises so that the tip of the ski forms a pie-shaped angle with the

snow. The leg should be lifted just enough to get the ski off the snow and turned.

2. Stiffening the body to resist the drag caused by the tip results in a jerky turn. Relax, allowing the body to be turned.

3. Excessive leaning to the inside of the turn will result in a dramatic crash when the edges are changed. Emphasize standing upright and directly over the spinning ski and boot.

ONE SKI 360 SPIN

The One Ski 360 Spin should be mastered before attempting the remaining stunts in this section. All succeeding stunts are a variation of this basic maneuver. Again, start with a turn into the hill so falls won't be too dramatic or bruising.

DESCRIPTION

Starting in a traverse at a moderate speed, the skier pushes off the outside/downhill ski in a skating motion, transferring all the weight to the inside ski. The ankle and knee of the weighted ski drive forward and to the inside of the turn to initiate the carving action of the ski. The outside ski is raised off the snow. The ski is turned uphill until it is pointed directly uphill or a little beyond. The upper body still pivots ahead of the

OUTRIGGER 360 SPIN

skis in an anticipated position. This is the critical point. The knee is rolled over the ski to decrease edging while maintaining forward pressure. The ski tip will seek the fall-line, and is aided by planting the outside pole. Anticipation and rotation of the leg by muscular action also help to complete the spin.

LEARNING STEPS

1. Review Finishing a One Ski Spin (page 65).

2. On flat terrain, practice rolling the supporting knee from side to side while maintaining a slight forward pressure on the ball of your foot.

3. Practice an uphill turn on the inside ski, working toward getting the ski tip to aim straight up the hill or beyond. Stop and plant both poles for support. Practice rolling the knee over to flatten the ski on the snow while maintaining forward pressure and looking in the direction of the turn. Using the outside pole, push off to complete the spin.

4. Try a complete 360 Spin. Wind up the upper body and then rapidly rotate the body in the direction of the turn to help initiate the spin.

5. As your skill increases, initiate a parallel turn and finish with a 360 Spin. Also try it on the outside foot. This is an excellent test of balance.

ERROR CORRECTION

1. Avoid leaning. Stay right over the turning ski to prevent sudden and unex-pected crashes caused by edges catching on the snow because they were not released.

2. There is a tendency to face the ski tip when it is turned uphill. The upper body must be anticipated beyond this point. Keep rotating the upper body in the direction of the turn to assist the turning of the ski.

3. Fear usually causes bending over at the waist in order to get closer to the snow. If you give in to this habit, you will be closer to the snow than you want to be. Emphasize standing upright with the back straight and the hips directly over the ski boots while looking in the direction of the turn.

4. Stiffening of the ankle makes it difficult to negotiate changes in the terrain and edging. Flex your ankle and knees slightly to allow more lateral movement of the leg.

OUTRIGGER 360 SPIN

The Outrigger 360 Spin is merely a One Ski 360 Spin started and ended in an Outrigger position. The extended leg is held off the snow and to the side in a High Outrigger position during the spin.

DESCRIPTION

Beginning in a Low Outrigger position with most of the weight on the inside ski, the upper body winds up with a counter-movement opposite to the direction of the spin as some weight is transferred to

the extended downhill ski. Then by actively pushing off the downhill ski, the upper body twists rapidly in the direction of the spin as the weight is transferred to the inside ski. The spin is done in the High Outrigger position (similar to the One Ski 360 Spin) with the extended leg held off the snow. The upper body is twisted ahead of the turning ski, with the head looking and leaning to the inside of the spin to balance the extended leg. When the spin is completed, the skier sinks back into a Low Outrigger position.

LEARNING STEPS

1. Practice One Ski 360 Spins. Lower your body during the spin to a High Outrigger position and lean to the inside for balance as the raised leg is extended to the side and held off the snow. At the completion of the spin, sink into a Low Outrigger position.

2. In a Stationary Outrigger position, practice shifting your weight from the inside ski to the extended ski as the upper body winds up to prepare for the rapid push-off of the extended ski to initiate the turn. The hips should become centered between the two skis during the windup. Then, on the initiation, the hips move rapidly back over the inside ski by pushing vigorously off the outside ski as the body unwinds.

3. Practice the initiation in an Outrigger traverse. Increase your speed so the spin will be easier. Then start the Outrigger

ROYAL 360 SPIN

360 at the end of an Outrigger Turn. You should spin all the way around ending in a Low Outrigger position.

ERROR CORRECTION

1. Frequently skiers think the ski remains on the snow during the spin, similar to a regular Outrigger Turn. This is not the case. Keep the ski extended to the side and off the snow.

2. Note that this maneuver is different from many of the other spins since you must lean to the inside to counterbalance for the weight of the extended leg. In most other maneuvers, try to stay centered over the weighted ski.

3. During the initiation, make a definite weight transfer from ski to ski. This can be aided by shifting the hips over the weighted inside ski during the spin.

ROYAL 360 SPIN

The Royal 360 requires strength to keep the raised ski off the snow and behind the hip during the spin. The high body position makes the stunt even more difficult because the upper body must counterbalance the weight of the raised ski with forward and backward, as well as lateral movements. Fear of moving backwards in a Royal Christie position also causes hesitation on the part of many students.

DESCRIPTION

The Royal 360 is initiated by turning uphill in the Royal Christie position with more pressure on the front of the ski,

turning until the ski faces straight uphill or farther. Then, maintaining the forward pressure on the ball of the foot, the knee is rolled over the ski to release the edge and flatten the ski on the snow, causing the tip to slide downhill. The outside pole is planted to assist the spin and balance. The body is anticipated and looks in the direction of the turn. As the second half of the turn is completed, rise while gradually decreasing forward pressure on the front of the ski. Lower the raised ski to the snow and resume a new traverse.

LEARNING STEPS

1. Review Finishing a One Ski Spin in the Royal Christie position. Maintain a balanced body position in a Royal position by bending both knees and holding the raised ski boot as close to the hips as possible. If the snow is soft, practice falling in this position with both knees bent. This will help overcome a fear of landing in a vulnerable position. Remember to keep the knees bent for the greatest amount of flexibility.

2. Review planting the outside pole when the spinning ski is pointed straight up the hill. Push with it against the snow in the direction of the spin to assist the spin and help the upper body anticipate while looking in the direction of the turn.

3. Review rolling the knee laterally to increase and decrease edging. Maintain forward pressure during the entire sequence.

4. Try the maneuver at a reasonable speed on a smooth, convex slope.

ERROR CORRECTION

1. Difficulty in the Royal 360 can usually be attributed to basic weaknesses in One Ski 360 Spins or leaning to the inside while in a Royal Christie position. These stunts should be practiced diligently until they can be done with a minimum of excess movement.

2. Leaning to the inside during initiation makes lateral knee movements and the resulting edge change difficult. Leaning is often caused by extending the raised foot to the side rather than directly behind the hip. Bending at the waist will help to bring the foot in behind the hip and keep the weight forward. Stand directly over the spinning ski or the "Snowsnake" will strike and you'll bite the snow.

3. The upper body should always be turned in the direction of the spin into an anticipated position to provide a base for the leg muscles to pull against to help turn the ski.

CROSSOVER 360 SPIN

Almost as easy as a One Ski 360 Spin, the Crossover 360 enables the skier to keep the raised ski boot close to or under the hips, making it easy to balance over the spinning ski. Fear of falling in this position hinders most skiers from attempting the stunt. But if the legs remain bent when falling, there is very little danger involved in this position.

CROSSOVER 360 SPIN

DESCRIPTION

To begin the Crossover 360, the weight is shifted to the downhill ski. The uphill ski is lifted forward and the tail is crossed over the front of the downhill ski so the tip of the raised ski is pointing uphill. With the skis crossed in this position, a One Ski 360 Spin is initiated on the downhill ski by turning into the hill with increased forward pressure and edging. The upper body pivots ahead of the spinning ski in an anticipated position. After turning more than 180 degrees, the raised inside ski is turned toward the original direction of travel. Then step out of the crossed position in a skating motion by pushing off the weighted outside ski. Land on the inside ski pointed in the

original direction of travel. The outside/downhill ski is brought in parallel to the other ski. This method of completing the Crossover 360 is most commonly used to complete Ballet routines, although there are many ways to complete this maneuver.

LEARNING STEPS

1. First, learn how to fall in a crossover position. Try falling uphill on your hip, back, or side. You will learn that it is possible to fall in this position without getting hurt as long as you remember to bend your knees and keep your arms in close. Then traverse slowly and practice falling.

2. Practice crossing and uncrossing in

a traverse to develop balance while the raised leg is changing positions. Try to remain flat-footed while the pressure shifts from the ball to the heel of the foot.
3. Practice the end of the spin first. It will teach you a way to get out of the maneuver once you are in it.
4. Finally, do the whole stunt.

ERROR CORRECTION

1. Beginning skiers typically remain with their weight back and never apply forward pressure to start the turn. Be sure to emphasize leaning backward to counterbalance the forward raising of the uphill ski when crossing the tail over the other ski. Then resume a flat-footed

balanced position with the body erect before initiating the 360 Spin. Avoid staying back on your heels.
2. Again, avoid leaning to the inside or bending at the waist. Keep your hips over the spinning ski and look in the direction of the turn.

There are other types of 360 Spins. Some are done in the air. Others require a certain part of the body to touch the snow. Most are variations of the maneuvers already explained here, and reflect the personal style of the performer. If you closely analyze what the Freestyler is doing, you may be able to master several new tricks using the skills described here.

5
FLEXIBILITY STUNTS

A flexibility stunt either looks painful, impossible, or as if the Freestylist's body is being stretched completely out of joint. Yet very little undue stress is placed on the muscles, tendons, and ligaments surrounding the Freestylist's joints if the maneuvers are done correctly. Most students can learn these maneuvers easily by following a step-by-step progression.

A few individuals, due to natural limitations in a specific joint, may find some stunts more difficult to learn than others. The authors are good examples. The one who is slightly pigeon-toed finds Legbreakers quite easy, but has a real struggle with the Shea-Guy. The other performs Shea-Guys easily but avoids Legbreakers. As you might expect, his feet turn naturally outward at the toes. Flexibility can be increased by participating in a program of stretching exercises. But an individual will still find it easier to do some things better than others. This also applies to one-sidedness. People are generally one-sided. They tend to spin in one direction, use the same hand, and step off the same leg if they have a

choice. Most people do this automatically and are quite unconscious of their side preference, which is not always related to right- or left-handedness.

Crossing over or holding a certain position requires skill in balancing on one ski. Consequently, the body and ski must be positioned in such a manner as to counterbalance the movements or location of the other ski.

Another primary skill is determining where the skis should be positioned to complete each maneuver with a minimum of stress and strain on the body. As a general rule, if you feel as if you're being ripped apart, you are either doing some portion of the stunt incorrectly or your body won't bend that way. Therefore, carefully analyze the stunt and try again, or avoid it altogether.

CROSSOVER
(Uphill Stepover)

The key to pulling this maneuver off successfully is angling the raised ski with respect to the running ski. The angle should be similar to a pie shape. The shorter your legs or longer your skis, the wider the pie shape must be.

DESCRIPTION

In a traverse position the weight is shifted to the uphill ski. The downhill ski is rocked back and then up forward to assist lifting motion. The downhill ski is kicked up in front, crossed over the uphill ski, and placed down on the snow at an angle to the uphill ski. The weight is immediately transferred to the "crossed over" ski by moving the hips and head over that ski. The arms should be forward. The new downhill ski is raised off the snow by pushing the ski tip out to the side in a circular motion while bending the knee. The raised ski continues to swing uphill and is placed on the snow parallel to the other ski.

CROSSOVER

LEARNING STEPS

1. Practice the Crossover in a stationary position. First try it with one ski on, then with both. Rock the downhill ski forward and back to assist the lift. Step over and place the ski on the snow at an approximately 30-degree angle to the other. Plant both poles for support and bend forward at the waist to assist lifting the other ski up and behind to uncross.

2. Practice the entire maneuver in a very slow traverse. Increase speed as proficiency develops.

ERROR CORRECTION

1. Skiers commonly hesitate to step on the uphill ski once it has been crossed over and placed on the snow. It is like a swimmer testing the water temperature with his big toe before diving in. Emphasize stepping immediately onto the crossed ski, transferring all the weight so the uncrossing can begin. Hesitation will usually cause loss of control and a crash will result.

2. During the last phase of the maneuver, the uncrossing, the raised tip sometimes catches on the snow. Practice standing still while twisting the raised leg and foot to create a circular swing of the ski back uphill. Lack of this action and failure to step into a pie shape usually cause the most difficulties during first attempts.

3. Avoid excessive forward lean or

pressure on the ball of the foot once the skis have been crossed. Otherwise, the ski will begin to turn uphill.

4. If the ski tip catches while uncrossing, bend the raised knee sharply.

CROSSBEHIND
(Reverse Crossover)

The Crossbehind involves exactly the opposite movements of the Uphill Crossover. Generally these two stunts can be learned at the same time. However, the

Crossbehind requires a little better balance.

DESCRIPTION

From a traverse, the uphill ski is lifted off the snow, swinging the ski tip in a circular motion uphill and back, allowing the upper body to twist slightly in the same direction. The raised ski boot is pulled into the hips by bending the knee. The leg and foot turn at the same time to swing the ski tip downhill. Face downhill and look for the tip. The ski is set on

CROSSBEHIND ·

the snow and immediately weighted, lifting the other ski off the snow. Rock back on the heel of the foot to assist raising the other ski in front as it is uncrossed. Then place it down parallel to the other ski in a new traverse position.

LEARNING STEPS

1. Practice in a stationary position with just the uphill ski on. The most critical and difficult movement is pulling the knee in and turning the leg and foot to make the tip swing downhill.

2. Next try it with both skis on. Stand on a small hill in order to make it easier to clear the tip of the swinging ski as it crosses behind. Plant both poles in front for support during the critical knee bend, turning of the leg and foot, and swing the tip downhill.

3. Then try the maneuver slowly across the hill without upsetting the continuity of movement. Work toward performing the stunt smoothly.

ERROR CORRECTION

1. Don't turn the upper body excessively uphill as the ski tip swings uphill. It is wasted motion and makes swinging the ski tip downhill a difficult task. Keep upper body movements to a minimum.

2. If you catch the ski tip on the snow when turning the leg and foot, you should bend the raised knee sharply. If

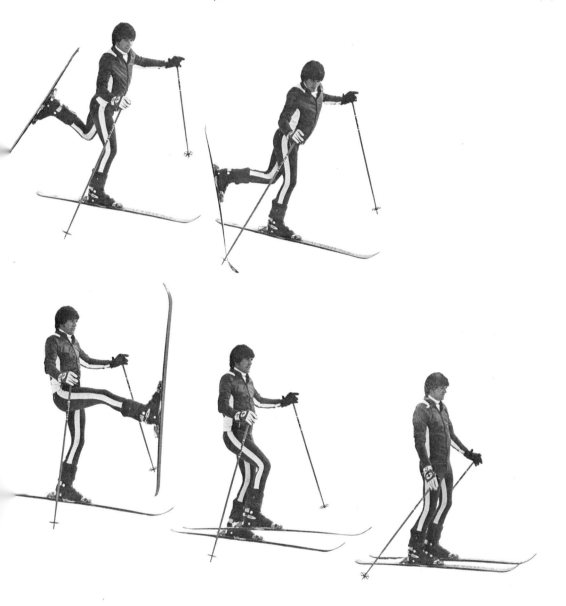

FALL-LINE CROSSOVER

the tip catches, you'll do a nose crash.

3. If you hesitate to step immediately onto the new downhill ski, you risk a fall. It is best to get into an upright position immediately so that unusual terrain changes won't cause a crash.

4. If balance seems to be a problem, close your eyes and concentrate on standing flat-footed, maintaining pressure over the sole of the whole foot. This exercise helps prevent leaning off balance.

FALL-LINE CROSSOVER
(Downhill Stepover)

This is similar to the Uphill Crossover, except you are going to step downhill into the fall-line. The stunt requires a little more courage because speed increases and you have farther to fall. Many times this stunt is used as an ending or a preliminary stunt in combination with other maneuvers.

DESCRIPTION

Beginning in a traverse position, all the weight is shifted to the downhill ski. The uphill ski is lifted. The upper body faces downhill as the raised ski is crossed over the front of the downhill ski. With a slight push off the downhill ski, the uphill ski is hopped over the downhill ski and lands straight down the fall-line or a little beyond. The weight is immediately shifted to the ball of the foot and the knee is driven to the inside to carve a

LEGBREAKER

short radius turn. The new uphill ski is lifted off the snow by bending the knee. The raised ski tip swings to the outside in a circular motion by turning the leg and placing it parallel to the other ski in a new traverse position.

LEARNING STEPS

1. Practice the steps standing still on flat terrain with only one ski on. Then use both skis. Move to a gentle slope and start all over again from a standstill position.

2. Then try the total maneuver from a

very slow traverse. Commit yourself to a strong initiation, hopping aggressively over the downhill ski.

ERROR CORRECTION

1. Skiers frequently land with their weight on the heel of the foot and fail to flex the ankle and knee to complete the turn. Leap over the downhill ski, reaching far downhill and planting both poles for support to assist balancing, and emphasize getting forward to help carve a turn.

2. If you hop to the inside of the turn,

you will crash in a dramatic belly flop ending in a frog position when the tip of the other ski catches and throws you to the snow. Keep the body centered over the "hopped" ski.

LEGBREAKER

The term "Legbreaker" makes the maneuver sound dangerous. When done quickly, it looks as if the legs could easily become tangled. In reality, the stunt doesn't require exceptional flexibility, but a simple placing of the skis in the correct spot while stepping from one ski to the other.

DESCRIPTION

Starting in a traverse, the uphill ski is weighted. The downhill ski is raised up behind the body with the ski tip pointing to the rear. The upper body starts turning uphill as the raised ski tip is lowered to the snow. A quick hopping off the uphill ski is followed by a rapid downhill twisting of the downhill raised leg as the ski tip drags, causing the raised ski to land on the snow parallel to the other ski

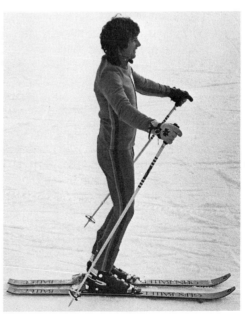

(which is now off the snow) with the ski tip pointing to the rear. By leaning back at the ankle, arching the back, and allowing the rotation of the upper body to continue, the uphill ski is lifted over the front of the downhill ski, swinging the ski tip in a circular motion downhill. The upper body continues to turn in the same direction. The ski is placed down on the snow pointing forward. The uphill ski is lifted and swung in a circular motion downhill over the tail of the downhill ski until it is also pointing forward in the original direction of travel in a new traverse position.

LEARNING STEPS

1. Remove both skis and practice the turning-stepping movements until you develop a feel for each individual step. This exercise provides a warm-up for the muscles before they are subjected to the stretching and twisting demanded by the maneuver.

2. Put on the downhill ski. Practice the lift, tip drag, and twisting the leg downhill so the ski points to the rear. Try to keep the ankles and knees bent to assure maximum flexibility. Place the turned ski quite a distance downhill from the uphill foot to allow greater flexibility for those who have difficulty turning their feet inward because of a natural limitation at the hip joint.

3. Now put on both skis and try it standing still. If the skis keep getting caught on the snow, try hopping to accentuate the stepping.

4. Try the stunt while moving slowly in a traverse. Work on continuity, increasing the speed of each stepping motion until the steps become hops. Gradually increase the speed of the traverse.

ERROR CORRECTION

1. If you experience difficulty when starting the maneuver, think about stepping into a Royal Christie position before the ski tip is lowered to the snow. Then you can begin facing uphill.

2. Many skiers have difficulty main-taining a pigeon-toed stance even for a brief instant. However, if the downhill ski is set on the snow a substantial distance from the uphill ski and then stepped on (like a person stepping backwards down a staircase with huge wide steps), then it is easier to hold the Leg-breaker position.

3. If you experience difficulty lifting the uphill ski off the snow, emphasize hopping backwards onto the downhill ski. This movement develops a flowing action where one movement assists the lifting, swinging action of the uphill ski.

SHEA-GUY

The Shea was invented by Mike Shea, a professional Freestyle skier from New York. It is a position that requires the ability to rotate the legs outward at the hip similar to standing in a "duckwalk" position. Once the position has been mastered, turns can be carved from side to side.

DESCRIPTION

Standing on one ski, the other ski is lifted off the snow. The raised ski is swung back behind the body crossing it over the other ski so it is placed on the snow with the tip pointing to the rear. The ski tips are now pointing in opposite directions with the weight on the inside edge of the ski pointing forward. The other ski is dragged on its inside edge and is used for balance. In a Low Shea, the knee of the dragging ski leg is actually in contact with the snow. When this maneuver is performed across the hill, the dragging ski is downhill and weight stays on the uphill ski. Turns can be done in the Shea by changing the edge of the weighted ski by rocking the upper body, hips, and weighted knee in the direction of the turn.

LEARNING STEPS

1. First try the Shea in a stationary position with skis pointing across the hill.

Face the hips and upper body uphill. Put all weight on the downhill ski and lift the uphill ski. Swing the raised ski to the rear and over the tail of the weighted ski. Place the raised ski on the snow parallel and downhill to the weighted ski. The skis should be pointed in opposite directions and about one to two feet apart. The upper body faces forward and the arms are used for balance. This is the High Shea position. A Low Shea position is a true test of knee and hip flexibility. Work down to it in steps until the knee of the rear ski is actually touching the snow. Some people cannot do this because of limited flexibility at the hip and knee joint. Determine your flexibility limits and stay within them. Avoid pushing your joints to the point of pain.

2. Before going any farther, get used to the Shea position by skiing across the hill at a very slow rate of speed. Gradually increase speed.

3. Begin working toward the fall-line until the position can be held while going straight down the hill.

4. On a very gentle slope, head down the fall-line and rock from side to side on the weighted ski, changing edges as you go. Keep the weight forward so the ski will begin carving a turn.

5. As skill increases, move to a steeper slope.

ERROR CORRECTION

1. The most common error in the Shea is being unable to hold an edge with the uphill ski. Weight must be on the uphill ski and the knee should move slightly uphill to hold an edge. If you start in a position that is too low, it will cause the knee to shift downhill, the ski to flatten, and slipping to begin. Don't rush into the Low Shea. Work on the high position; the Low Shea will come gradually.

2. Balance can be another problem. The arms can be used to counterbalance the position of the lower body, with the dragging leg providing a very small degree of support.

3. Avoid bending at the waist. Doing so causes the hips to move away from their

SHEA-GUY: HIGH AND LOW

place of balance. Keep the upper body over the hips and as close to the weighted ski as possible.

Remember, it isn't always possible for each individual to do every maneuver described here. Differences in body build and the location of muscle attachments to bones may cause a natural limitation of flexibility. Work on exercises to promote flexibility after a thorough warm-up. *Flexibility can be gained through gentle stretching exercises over a long period of time.* If, after many months of work, a certain position is still beyond your range of movement, leave it out of your routine. Substitute something else. There are many other things to learn that are just as impressive and difficult to perform.

6

SNOW CONTACT STUNTS

Snow Contact Stunts are maneuvers in which the body touches the snow, using it for support and/or to assist the completion of a roll. Some of the maneuvers may have developed when falling skiers tried to come up skiing instead of landing in a big pile. We're sure some skier caught his tips, flipped over head first, hit the snow, rolled up to his skis, and continued down the mountain with a big smile. Then other daredevils began copying these antics and invented their own methods of recovery skiing. Bruises and sprains were common. Speed seemed to be a necessity and made the snow even harder than it looked. Many smart skiers learned most of these stunts on soft snow, but "hot" skiers had to do them on packed slopes, many times in moguls. Through much trial and error, easier ways were found to learn the stunts and reduce the smashing, bone-rattling impact characteristic of Snow Contact Stunts.

PRELIMINARY PRACTICE

Most Snow Contact Stunts can be easily related to movements in gymnastics. Get a tumbling mat or select a soft spot on

some grass and begin learning a forward roll, a kip-up, a shoulder roll, and a diving forward roll. Successful completion of each of these maneuvers depends upon landing on the right place in the right way in order to avoid exposing the head, neck, shoulder, and back to injury.

Another demand of Contact Stunts is learning to reduce the falling or rolling impact of the body on the snow. The higher you fall, the more you'll feel it. But if your body is closer to the snow, there is less distance to fall, reducing the force of the impact. Add speed before you've learned and you may add pain. Start slowly and learn correctly. Learn to roll on the snow in the direction of travel. Avoid flat landings. Learn exactly where your body goes, what you land on, and how to roll up. Think of the analogy of a rock skipping across water. The rock hits the water with a glancing blow and bounces off. If it hits more directly, it goes straight to the end of its journey.

Avoid sticking your arms out to prevent falling. They may get stuck in the snow. That's an unpleasant situation if you're ten yards down the hill from where your arms caught. In stunts where the

skis are lifted off the snow, it is important to bring the ski boots under and close to the hips before landing. The tucked position facilitates standing up after the maneuver is completed. The importance of this point can be well illustrated if you put your skis on and practice many of the stunts on soft grass before attempting them on the snow. Such practice also emphasizes how you must turn your legs in order to avoid banging the tails of the skis on the grass. This prevents the typical error in which the skier ends a roll by jamming both tails into the snow, abruptly stopping the maneuver.

After learning the basic tumbling stunts, practice them again with poles, but never strap them on. Learn proper placement so you won't land on them. Then try the stunts again with skis but without poles. Finally try the stunts again with both poles and skis. Whatever you do, learn the stunts on soft grass or a padded surface before trying them on snow.

When practicing on snow, wear a

DIVING FORWARD ROLL

parka or windshirt, something that snow won't stick to. Sweaters can easily become encrusted with snow, resulting in an appearance resembling the Abominable Snowman. Tuck in all shirt tails to prevent snow from getting up your back. A one-piece suit is ideal for this type of practice. Remember, keep the pole straps off and unhook your runaway straps If you're practicing in a protected trick area. You don't want a windmilling ski to hit you, but neither do other skiers enjoy your skis sticking in their body.

Look for soft snow. Avoid hard-packed snow or ice for first attempts. Practice at zero miles per hour first and increase speed as skill improves. After one good fall, go back to the basics. Bruises and pain can be substantially reduced with systematic practice.

THE LAYBACK

The Layback is a good warm-up exercise, and an excellent beginning maneu-

LAYBACK

ver that teaches how to land softly on snow while getting the poles out of the way. The Layback requires considerable thigh and abdominal strength.

DESCRIPTION

Skiing down the fall-line the arms are raised straight over the head and the poles point to the sky. Sit on the tails of the skis by bending at the knees and hips, then lie down on the skis. The poles point to the rear and the chin is tucked against the chest. This is the Layback position. To get up, the arms are brought forward to assist rolling up. The poles may be planted for further assistance.

LEARNING STEPS

1. Try the Layback first while standing still on flat terrain.
2. Sit on the tails of the skis while moving and try to get up.
3. Then do the stunt straight down a well-packed smooth hill.

ERROR CORRECTION

1. Remember to keep the poles overhead to avoid hitting your face on the pole handles if you unfortunately allowed the poles to get in front of you.
2. Frequently skiers have difficulty getting up because their hips are away from their boots. Keep your hips as close as you can to your ski boots to assist standing.

THE ROLLOVER
(Worm Turn)

A Rollover is simply two consecutive Layback positions connected by a roll over sideways. It can be done down the fall-line or from a traverse by rolling downhill.

DESCRIPTION

Skiing down the fall-line, lower to a Layback position with the poles overhead and pointed uphill. Then roll sideways over onto your stomach, keeping your

ski boots close to your hips to prevent the tips from catching. Your head should always be off the snow. Continue rolling in the same direction to another Layback position, standing up to finish.

LEARNING STEPS

1. Practice the whole maneuver standing still.
2. Do it first down a gentle slope.
3. Try the Rollover in a traverse. Roll sideways down the hill.

ERROR CORRECTION

1. Bumping the head is usually caused by not tucking the chin on the chest in the Layback position. When rolling over, the head must be lifted to prevent dragging on the snow.
2. To prevent the ski tips from catching on the snow during the roll and to assist standing up, the tails of the skis should be held next to the back during the roll.

THE SIDE ROLL

The Side Roll is a valuable lead-up exercise for learning Forward Rolls and Shoulder Rolls. The Side Roll emphasizes lowering your body before starting the roll, placing the poles out of the way, rounding the back, and keeping the boots next to the hips. This stunt is also used for avoiding embarrassing falls when overturning in deep or wet snow.

DESCRIPTION

Starting in a traverse down the hill, the skis are turned uphill, the edges set, and the body lowered. The hands are placed next to the boots with the poles pointing straight back and parallel to the skis. The back is rounded and the chin tucked when starting to roll sideways downhill onto the back. The boots are held as close to the hips as possible while rolling. The sideways momentum will complete the roll. A push with the uphill arm can be used to assist standing. The

THE ROLLOVER
(WORM TURN)

skis will land pointing more into the fall-line.

LEARNING STEPS

1. Try the Side Roll first while stationary. Lower your body by bending your ankles, knees, and hips, and rounding your back until your chest is resting on your thighs. Pay particular attention to placing the poles parallel and close to the skis to avoid landing on them. Then roll over.

2. Now try it at a very slow speed. Turn uphill before setting your edges and rolling.

3. Increase speed and aim more down the hill. Turn uphill and come almost to an abrupt stop by setting the edges before rolling.

4. Select a round mogul. Experiment with different ways to roll off moguls.

Turn uphill, set your edges, roll over the crest of the mogul or along its side.

5. In deep snow, turn hard uphill and roll sideways. Work into this exercise gradually. Keep increasing the speed until the roll can be done almost completely in the air. This exercise is an excellent lead-up stunt for a side somersault.

ERROR CORRECTION

1. The most common error is not turning uphill before trying to roll sideways. Skiers typically roll sideways while still aimed downhill. Sore shoulders and necks are a result. The original forward momentum is checked by turning the skis uphill at a right angle to the direction of travel, then the edge-set starts the body rolling sideways in line with the original direction of travel. This way the

SIDE ROLL

body rolls in the direction of the original forward momentum.

2. Don't begin the roll from an upright position. Lower your body before rolling. The snow seems very hard when toppling from a high position.

3. The location of the poles on the snow won't seem important until the first time you land on them. They should be kept parallel and next to the skis.

4. A tangled Worm Turn is caused by leaning back, which results in a crash landing on your stomach. When rolling, keep your body forward directly over your boots.

5. Typically during the completion of the roll, beginners allow their legs to extend slightly, making it extremely difficult to stand. Keep the boots adjacent to and under the hips when trying to stand.

COMPLETING ROLLS

To avoid broken skis and sprained muscles and joints, it is important to learn the end of a roll before learning the whole maneuver. Learning the end of a roll also helps to reduce fear substan-

tially because you only have to concentrate on one aspect of the maneuver, the beginning. Then when the first complete roll is attempted, so much time has been spent rolling up and tucking the head that rolling over doesn't seem to be as awesome. Confidence in the ability to end the roll will give you the courage to attempt it. Most rolls are completed by turning the legs to the side and rolling up, but a few rolls can also be finished with a "kip-up."

LEG-TURNING

To learn how to complete a roll using this method the poles should be set aside. Lie on your back with the legs pointing down a gentle hill. The skis are raised overhead by bending your knees, rounding your back, and lifting your hips until you are resting on your upper back. To roll up, the hips are lowered to the snow while the skis begin turning to one side keeping the boots as close to the hips as possible. The skis should land at approximately a right angle to the direction of the roll. The upper body lunges forward as the arms reach forward to get

LEG TURNING
ROLL-UP

over the skis. The lunging action will decrease as the speed of the roll increases, for momentum then carries the body up over the skis.

The most difficult part of this exercise is usually rolling into the starting position. It takes considerable abdominal strength. Of course the exercise can be practiced without being on snow—any grassy area will do. The roll-up exercise emphasizes turning the legs and skis so the tails of the skis won't catch, an important factor on snow. If the tails of the skis catch in the snow, they may break off. Try to roll down the length of your spinal column. This will also help with the initiation of various other rolls. Remember, when rolling, the legs are turning so the boots will land next to the hips with the skis pointing across the hill.

KIP-UP

This method of completing a roll is considerably more difficult than the leg-turning method, but allows the skis to remain pointing downhill. The timing of this maneuver is very critical. The kip-up requires greater abdominal strength to extend the hips off the snow in a forceful action so the boots can be snapped under the hips. Take a gymnastic lesson and learn a headspring and shoulder kip before trying the kip-up on snow. Short skis are recommended.

Again, this maneuver should first be attempted without poles. The legs are raised until the ski boots are well overhead and resting primarily on the shoulders with the hips well off the snow and the knees straight. From this position, roll forward until the base of the shoulder blades touch the snow. At this instant the snap-reach action of the kip is executed. The legs drive upward at an angle of 45–60 degrees with sufficient force to lift the body. When the legs and hips are fully extended, the back is arched and the knees bend rapidly so the feet can reach under the body for the snow.

Perhaps the most frequent mistake in attempting a kip-up is a tendency to let the legs rise gradually before the rapid

extension. The legs must be extended vigorously to initiate the snapping action. Rolling down so the lower back or hips contact the snow also reduces the snap-reach kipping action. Long skis also make it difficult since the tails tend to catch while the feet are reaching for the snow. Hours of practice are required to learn the timing of this skill.

FORWARD ROLL
(Monkey Roll, Queersprung)

The Forward Roll on snow is similar to a forward roll in gymnastics. The rolling actions are identical, the only differences are the positions from which the Forward Roll is initiated and the methods of coming out of it. During initiation, both ski tips can be pointed either in the same direction or in opposite directions across the hill. The roll can be completed by a leg-turning roll-up or by a kip-up. Each method involves slightly different skills. Your selection of the method of initiation and completion is determined by the placement of this stunt in a sequence of a routine. Commonly, Freestylers initiate this roll in a routine with their ski tips pointing in opposite directions and finish with a kip-up. The Forward Roll is also an excellent lead-up stunt for the Shoulder Roll.

DESCRIPTION
To initiate the maneuver, the ski tips are spread so they point in opposite directions. The spreading can be accomplished by doing a kick turn while in a traverse or by allowing the tips to spread

KIP-UP (COMPLETING ROLLS)

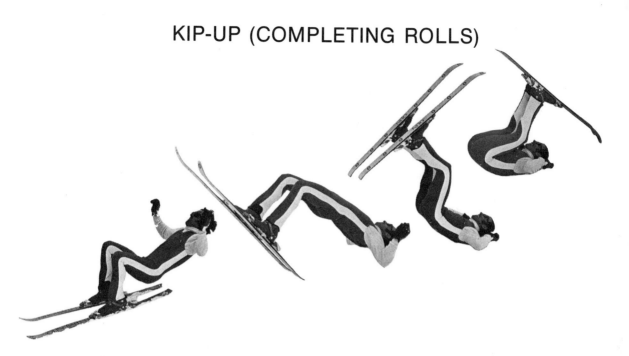

while running straight down the hill (inside edges catch to help initiate the roll), or from a Killer Kick position (see page 106). The body is lowered by bending the ankles, knees, and hips with the back rounded. The chin is tucked to the chest and the arms are extended toward the snow with poles pointing out to the side. Simultaneously, push forward off your feet so the hips come straight over the head. The knuckles of the hands should hit the snow first to take a little of the impact. The head and neck are tucked under so the major impact is taken on the rounded upper back. If a kip-up is used, then a rapid snap-reach action of the legs takes place before the hips come in contact with the snow. If a leg-turning roll-up is used, the ski boots are kept close to the hips during the rolling action. Then the skis are turned to one side to avoid catching the tails as the arms reach forward to assist standing.

LEARNING STEPS

1. Learn a Forward Roll without skis on. Then try it with only your poles. Your hands and knuckles should take very little impact. The roll is almost a somersault in the air, landing on your upper back. Try to start in a low position so you don't have too far to fall.

2. Review leg-turning roll-ups with skis on before making the first attempt. Remove poles. Try your first rolls with your skis pointing in the same direction. Face downhill with your upper body and get down on your hands and knees, skis across the hill, body pointed downhill. Raise your knees off the snow, lifting your hips. Push off with your feet rolling over onto your back. Finish the roll by turning the skis to the side. Do this several times, working on soft landings. Use your hands and a low roll to reduce the landing impact.

3. Now try the same thing with poles. Make sure they point straight out to the side away from the impact area.

4. Now stand. Crouch way down, twisting your body so it is facing downhill. Reach for the snow with your hands, placing them quite close to your downhill boot. The reaching action will help your body turn over. Give a push to start the roll, taking a little of the impact with your hands. Land on your upper back. Do a leg-turning roll-up. If the poles are a handicap at this stage of the learning, don't use them. As skill and confidence

FORWARD ROLL

increase, start from a higher position each time.

5. Now ski down the hill very slowly and abruptly turn the skis across the hill. Set your edges and stop. Face downhill and do a Forward Roll. Work toward blending the edge-set with the initiation of the Forward Roll, as one should flow into the other. Set the edges to create a rebound for springing into the Forward Roll.

6. To finish a Forward Roll with a kip-up, repeat the above procedure. A little more speed may be necessary for some skiers to assist the snap-reach action of the legs.

7. When attempting a series of Forward Rolls, keep the ski tips spread for the entire roll and landing.

ERROR CORRECTION

1. Digging the tails in at the end of the roll-up is a result of allowing the ski boots to get too far away from the hips and not turning the skis across the hill. The same thing occurs in a kip-up if the hips aren't lifted high enough to allow the feet to snap back under.

2. An unbalanced roll is a result of not rolling directly down the length of your spinal column. Try to land evenly on both sides of your back.

3. Landing on your neck or head can be caused by diving too far out. The head should be tucked down by the ski boots and to the chest as the hips are lifted over the head. Sometimes a failure to push off with the feet causes a toppling onto the head. Fear usually causes people to hesitate and avoid a vigorous push by the feet. Push with the feet hard

enough to somersault over and land on the upper back.

4. Difficulty in initiation while moving is usually caused by failing to set the edges. A stable platform is needed to spring from. Review edge-sets with a stop to work back into moving Forward Rolls.

5. When initiating from a Killer Kick position (page 106), the weight should be kept over the uphill ski so it is easier to roll downhill once the other ski is lowered to the snow. Frequently skiers tend to be on the uphill side of the uphill ski, making the initiation difficult. Then they have to lunge downhill with their upper body traveling a greater distance to start the roll.

SHOULDER ROLL

The Forward Roll is an excellent lead-up maneuver for the Shoulder Roll. They differ in only a few respects. During the Shoulder Roll the skier rolls diagonally across his back instead of straight down the spinal column. The uphill shoulder leads, bringing that same side of the back in contact with the snow first. Also, the downhill pole can be planted for support and as a visual guide for placing the upper back in the correct position.

DESCRIPTION

Starting from a traverse or the end of a turn, there is a quick dropping in the ankles and knees and setting of the edges. The inside/downhill pole is planted toward the fall-line near the heel of the downhill ski boot. With a spring in the legs, the uphill/outside hand, shoulder, and arm cross in front of the body, reaching for the heel of the downhill ski boot. The pole in this outside hand is laid next to and parallel to the downhill ski with the pole tip pointing toward the ski tips. The head looks for and drops toward the planted basket of the inside/downhill pole and is tucked under just before making contact with the snow. Snow contact is made on the outside upper back at the shoulder blade. The body rolls diagonally across the back, ending on the inside lower back or hip while the skis turn during the roll. The ski boots are kept close to the hips at the end of the roll to prevent catching the tails of the skis and to assist rolling up. The Shoulder Roll is completed when you are standing up and skiing off in the opposite direction.

LEARNING STEPS

1. Try a Shoulder Roll without skis or poles. Lower and turn your upper body downhill leading with the outside hand. Touch the snow near the heel of your foot. Push off with your feet, tucking your head and rolling across the outside upper back diagonally to the inside hip. Continue practicing until enough confidence develops to initiate a roll in this twisted position.

2. Learn with one pole at a time. Remove the straps. Use the outside pole first. Bring it across the front of your body, laying it down with the pole tip

SHOULDER ROLL

aimed in the same direction as the feet. Place your hand near the heel of the downhill ski boot. Then roll.

3. The inside pole is planted out to the side near the heel of your downhill ski boot. It is used for momentary support during the edge-set and initiation. Bring the uphill/outside hand across and down between the planted pole and the heel of your boots. Drop your head and shoulder toward the basket. Push with your feet, tucking your head and roll. When the roll is mastered with a single pole, repeat, using both poles.

4. Put the poles aside when making your first attempts with skis on. Face across the hill and put your downhill hand on the snow for support. Reach across your body with the uphill/outside hand, putting it between the supporting hand and the heel of the downhill ski boot. Push with your feet. Tuck your head and try to place the uphill/outside shoulder blade as close to the supporting hand as possible to initiate the diagonal roll. Don't forget to turn your legs so your skis land pointing in the opposite direction.

5. Then try the whole maneuver from a stationary position using poles. Remember the lower you are to the snow, grass, or mat, the less your impact will be.

6. On the snow, review the roll in a stationary position. Select a soft practice spot. Start from a higher body position each time and work for continuity when settling from a high position to the lower position to start the roll.

7. Now ski down the hill very slowly. Abruptly turn the skis uphill, set the edges, and stop. Plant the downhill pole

in the fall-line near the heel of the downhill ski boot. Reach across, lowering yourself and do a Shoulder Roll. Try to blend the edge-set with the initiation of the roll. One should lead into the other without a break in the continuity. The edges must be set to provide a platform to spring and initiate the roll. Repeat the maneuver, increasing speed to create a more forceful edge-set and greater spring. A more forceful edge-set will provide a stronger initiation, which could eventually lead to doing the complete roll in the air without touching the back to the snow. However, when attempting to complete the roll in the air, find a soft place to practice.

ERROR CORRECTION

1. Landing on the midline of the back rather than on one side is usually a result of failing to reach far enough toward the heel of the downhill ski boot with the outside hand. Try to put your head and outside shoulder on the snow near the basket of the downhill ski pole.

2. Diving too far out makes it difficult to land on the upper back and roll. It is better to drop the head close to the boots and push the hips out over the head. The farther you dive out, the faster you have to be going to complete the roll in the air.

3. If the tails of the skis are sticking in the snow, turn the skis to the side by turning the legs and pulling the ski boots close to and under the hips at the completion of the roll. Typically, skiers relax once they have the roll started because they feel the worst part is over. Well, actually it is, but the stunt must be finished. So the boots and skis must be kept under the hips upon landing.

4. Difficulty in initiation is usually caused by lack of an edge-set. A solid platform is needed from which to spring. Both edges must be set, springing off both feet to initiate the roll.

5. Terrain can aid or hinder the roll. Steep hills are softer than flat. The impact of the landing is substantially reduced because of the steeper landing surface. The body tends to bounce or skip off easier. Rolling over moguls can almost eliminate landing on your back. The roll can be done almost completely in the air. The edges can be set near the crest of the mogul (but not on it), planting the downhill pole on the crest. Then roll over the top of the mogul. The body should barely touch the snow on the steep side of the mogul.

KILLER KICK
(Outrigger Kick Turn)

A combination of two Outrigger positions and a kick turn, this maneuver is difficult for some individuals because of their naturally limited range of movement at the hip joint. Those who have difficulties doing simple kick turns or who are pigeon-toed will encounter problems with this maneuver.

DESCRIPTION
From a Low or High Outrigger position, the upper body and hip turn more downhill as the back is lowered to the snow directly over the uphill weighted ski. The extended downhill/inside leg is raised high, then turned so the ski is pointing across the fall-line in the opposite direction. It is lowered to the snow and imme-

KILLER KICK

diately weighted. The knee is bent so the edge can bite in the snow and prevent the ski from slipping sideways. With the edge holding, the skier pushes off the uphill ski to shift weight over the downhill ski. The upper body is brought over the newly weighted ski with the center of the chest over the knee. The outside/uphill ski is dragged around in a circular patch so it becomes the extended downhill ski in a new Outrigger position headed in the opposite direction.

LEARNING STEPS

1. The Killer Kick should first be practiced in a stationary position. Precise timing is required to clear the extended ski off the snow so it can be turned. The first step is to review a simple kick turn. Bring the downhill leg up in front of the body, placing the tail of the downhill ski on the snow. Turn the leg and ski so the ski tip swings downhill and lands on the snow with the downhill ski pointing in the opposite direction. Complete the kick turn by assuming an Outrigger position.

2. Now repeat the simple kick turn, but begin by lowering your hips to the tail of the uphill ski as you raise your downhill ski to turn it. Sit lower and lower before beginning to raise the leg. Extend it to the side in an Outrigger position to assist clearing the tail of the ski from the snow.

3. Once the extended leg has been lowered to its new position, practice lunging forward over it. From a position on your back, bend forward abruptly at the waist, lifting the upper body off the snow. Reach forward with your arms and try to get your head over your legs. Push off the inside edge of the uphill/outside ski. This action coupled with the forward momentum will raise your body over the new inside ski.

4. Now practice the maneuver while moving slowly. Keep the hips and back

over the weighted ski while lifting and turning the extended ski. As speed increases, momentum increases. As a result, the rocking-up lunging action of the body will decrease, requiring less strength in assuming the new Outrigger position.

ERROR CORRECTION

1. Failing to lean back on the snow makes it difficult to lift the other ski and turn it. Try to lower yourself while lifting the extended leg.

2. Stopping is a result of too little speed or dragging too long on the snow. Once the skill has been mastered, go faster to make it easier to stand up.

3. Difficulty in rising over the new inside ski can be caused by laying too far uphill while raising and turning the extended leg. When in doubt, lay the hips and downhill shoulder blade right on the tail of the uphill ski.

4. Failure to set the edge in the snow results in ski slippage. Correct this by

HIP 360 SPIN

raising the knee slightly so the edge will bite. Then it will hold and there will be something solid to stand on. Reach forward with your arms to help get body weight moving up over the edged ski.

5. Catching the tail of the raised ski is caused by not lifting the ski high enough before turning the leg. Swing the raised ski high off the snow.

HIP 360 SPIN
(Sitting Spin)

The Hip 360 Spin requires balancing on one hip while spinning. Everything else is off the snow. The snow should be firmly packed to prevent sinking in during the spin. The hip can be placed on the snow from a low position so as to scarcely feel the impact.

DESCRIPTION

Starting in a High Outrigger position with most of the weight on the inside ski, prepare for the spin by winding up the upper body with a countermovement opposite to the direction of the spin as some weight is transferred to the extended downhill ski. Then actively push off the downhill ski, rapidly twisting the upper body in the direction of spin while lowering the hip to the snow. As soon as the

hip touches, rock slightly back to help lift the skis off the snow while looking in the direction of the spin. The knees are bent to bring the boots and skis closer to the hips to increase the speed of the spin. When the spin is completed, the skis are lowered to the snow to assume a standing position.

LEARNING STEPS

1. Try hip spinning on a waxed floor to find out where you spin best. Remember that when wearing boots and skis you will have to rock slightly back to compensate for the added weight.

2. On the snow, practice the end of the spin first. Sit on the snow. Point your ski tips uphill. Rock back on just your inside hip. Lift your skis off the snow, bringing them toward your chest. Push with your hands and lean back in the direction of the spin. Practice finishing the spin several times before trying the whole maneuver.

3. During the initial attempt, select firm snow that is convex, or try the spin on the broad crest of a round mogul to help to clear your skis off the snow. Start the spin more uphill so you won't have as far to spin. Remember to push off actively and begin spinning before lowering yourself to the ground.

ERROR CORRECTION

1. Catching the tails of the skis on the snow is a result of not rocking back far enough on the hip to help with lifting the skis. Bend your knees, bringing the skis closer to your hips.

2. Spinning slowly can be caused by a weak initiation or by leaving the skis too far out to the side. A hard push off the outside ski and bringing the skis in for a faster spin will help correct this problem.

3. Tipping over sideways is a result of leaning too far to the inside during the initiation. Practice balancing on your hip to see where your balance point is located. Then lean inside just enough to compensate for the pull of centrifugal force.

Snow Contact Stunts can be bruising or enjoyable. It just depends on how you go about learning them. At times, the knowledge of these stunts can turn a potential disaster into a remarkable recovery. In competitive Ballet routines they are only used if the stunt fits in with the music and provides continuity from one stunt to the next. Practice is the key to success.

7

POLE STUNTS

Ski poles are used in a variety of ways in Freestyle skiing. In Stunt and Ballet, ski poles can create a visual effect of personal interpretation of the music or a maneuver. They may also be used as a support and work as an integral part of a stunt. Maneuvers that use the poles for support are called Pole Stunts. In all Pole Stunts, the palms of the hands are on the top of the poles. The fingers and thumb point down the shaft toward the baskets as they grasp the handle.

Pole Stunts are done on snow hard enough to prevent the baskets from breaking through the top layer of the snow while supporting the skier's weight. Yet the snow must be soft enough to cushion a fall. Usually these conditions do not exist at the same time. Practice Pole Stunts on the grass without skis before trying them on the snow. This will give you a feeling for the maneuver and teach you the basic mechanics. Leave the poles unstrapped so your wrists won't be injured if the poles catch in the ground. Pole tips can also cause damage. Either put rubber bumpers on the tips or avoid rugs, floors, and mats. Once you have a feel for the

maneuver, go to the mountain, locate some hard/soft snow, and give it a try.

TIP STAND

The Tip Stand is a stationary maneuver requiring excellent balance. You need a flat slope, hard snow, strong arms, and strong skis. Many ski tips have been broken learning this stunt, but if you are willing to take that chance, read on.

DESCRIPTION

One pole is planted between the two ski tips. The other pole is planted approximately three feet to the side. The ski that is between the two poles is lifted and its tip is set in the snow underneath the hips by flexing at the knee. Weight is put on the planted tip by pushing off with the arms and other foot. The planted ski's tail is rested against the upper back. More and more weight is placed on the planted ski until it is possible to maintain balance and lift the other ski off the snow. The tip of the newly raised ski is swung to the side and back placing it on the snow two to three feet from the other ski and under the hip. Once the tip is

TIP STAND (STEP-UP)

planted, the weight is shifted so it is balanced evenly on both skis. To return to a standing position, more weight is shifted to one side by pushing off the poles while the skis pivot on their tips and twist to the side.

LEARNING STEPS

1. First learn how to get out of a Tip Stand to avoid falling backwards and breaking your ski tips. Jump up, using the poles for support, and pivot to the side on the ski tips, landing on your feet. This is the easiest way to get out of a Tip Stand. If you encounter difficulty while pivoting, try to bring the ski boots close to the hips so the skis point almost straight down. Then push hard to the side to complete the pivot and landing.

2. Now get some friends to help you.

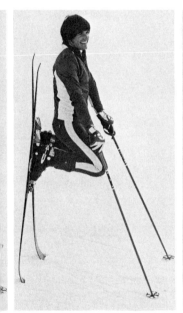

They should assist when you are trying to balance on one ski and two poles. The critical step is moving the second ski into position. Friends can steady your upper body to prevent falling forward on your head or tipping backwards.

3. Once a Tip Stand has been mastered, try a "press-up." To "press up" to a Tip Stand, the hips must be shifted forward to a point over the front of the ski tips and the poles planted. This is accomplished by springing up and forward at about a 45-degree angle while reaching with the arms. When full extension is reached, the weight is transferred to the poles, supporting most of your weight. Immediately bend at the knees and pull the ski boots to the hips. The tips of the skis catch on the snow as the tails are drawn up to the back. Some weight is

TIP STAND (PRESS-UP)

shifted to the tips of the planted skis so balance is maintained on all four points.
4. Another way to get down from a Tip Stand is to shift all your weight to one ski. Then lift the other ski off the snow and swing the tip out to the side and forward so it can be placed on the snow in its original position. Shift your weight to the ski that is flat on the snow. Lift the other ski tip off the snow and return it to its original position. This way requires the most balance and is the least graceful.
5. For variety, try "walking" on all fours. Get in a Tip Stand. Carefully lift one pole and move it forward. Then move the other pole. Now lift one ski and take a forward step. Repeat with the other ski. Continue "walking" until you collapse in a pile completely exhausted. If you are a master of balance, lift one pole, then the other, and remain balanced on only two skis for as long as you can.

ERROR CORRECTION

1. When getting up in a Tip Stand, placing the poles too far in front makes it difficult to shift the weight back onto the skis. The poles and arms are just balancing supports. The skis support most of the body weight. This changes when "walking," for then both skis and poles act as legs and carry their share of the weight.
2. When falling backwards, push hard on one pole and bend forward at the waist. This should cause the skis to pivot to the side and prevent broken ski tips.
3. When falling forward, twist and pivot your skis, landing on your feet or side. Or, lower yourself down to the snow, chest first, using your arms and poles for support.
4. Avoid placing the first ski too far behind you. It makes balancing difficult. The first ski should be placed directly under the hip so the skis will be perpendicular to the snow when in the Tip Stand position.

360 TIP ROLL

A 360 Tip Roll can be learned from a moving position, but if it is learned from a stationary position, the impact of a fall will be reduced.

DESCRIPTION

Facing across the hill, both poles are

planted downhill while the knees bend to prepare for a spring. Then actively leap into the air, twisting the body in the direction of the spin. As the upper body rises over the poles for support, the knees are bent, drawing the skis and boots in behind the hips. The tails of the skis almost touch the back and are perpendicular to the snow. The head leads the twisting action by looking over the inside shoulder. This is similar to pivoting out of a Tip Stand. There is a push off the poles to complete the twist and shift the weight back over the feet.

LEARNING STEPS

1. The 360 Tip Roll can be practiced first without skis on a grassy area. Remember to take the pole straps off. The trick in doing a 360 Tip Roll is getting the body high into the air and over the poles. When first beginning, plant the poles to the side and behind the heels of your ski boots so your hips and upper body are twisted to face the poles. Jump high over the poles, twisting the body in the direction of the spin. The poles provide support for additional "air time." Complete the twisting action by turning your feet to

the side and absorb the landing by bending your legs.

2. With skis on, try the following exercise, which emphasizes looking over the shoulder in the direction of the twist. The exercise can be thought of as a modified Tip Roll without poles. Sit on the tails of your skis. Roll downhill to a modified push-up position with your hands and ski tips on the snow while the knees are held off the snow. Keep your ski boots close to and behind your hips. Bend your elbows and push vigorously off with your hands, looking over your shoulder and rolling to the side until you are back on your skis. Try the exercise a few times, lunging onto and off your hands while looking hard over your shoulder. Remember to assume a low position at first.

3. When starting in a standing position, plant the poles two or three feet down the hill and behind the heels of your ski boots. Lean downhill over the poles with your upper body so your hands and arms are actually supporting some of the body weight. With a spring off the snow, turn your upper body over the poles so your chest is directly above the poles, using them for support. Bring the feet up close to the back of the hips. Keep looking

over your shoulder in the direction of the roll and allow your feet to fall downhill. As your feet reach the snow, push off the poles to a balanced position over the skis.

4. Continue to roll, trying to raise the upper body to an upright position during the twist. Use your arms as extensions of the poles to help keep the body upright. On each succeeding jump, twist the body a little more vigorously as you rise to the poles for support. Look over your shoulder to continue the twisting action. Eventually twist the body quite vigorously on the way up and look hard in the direction of the twist, bringing the boots in behind your hips. You will go all the way around.

5. A moving Tip Roll requires a slight turn uphill and a setting of the edges. The edge-set creates a stable platform for the vigorous spring. The poles are planted a little farther forward because the body will be traveling forward and downhill in the air. I hold the chest up for a higher Tip Roll. Once the moving Tip Roll is mastered, you will find it easier than a standing Tip Roll.

ERROR CORRECTION

1. The farther the poles are planted downhill and away from the skis, the more the maneuver becomes a low roll over the ski poles, which is an excellent lead-up maneuver. The experts plant the poles closer to the skis when they want a high upright Tip Roll, so that the center of the twist lies in their upper body and the poles are used for support and as an aid to continue the twisting action.

2. A common error is failing to look over the shoulder in the direction of the twist during the complete maneuver. Usually beginners will start by looking over their shoulder but then allow the head to rotate back so it faces straight ahead over their chest. Looking back and down the arm also causes the head to drop and the hips to tilt throwing the body alignment off. Look right over the shoulder for something that is in the distance. It helps to keep the head up.

3. Failing to complete a 360 Tip Roll can be caused by not bringing the ski boots into the hips, so that the skis are pointed straight down to the snow. This error also causes a slower twisting action.

540 TIP ROLL

A 540 Tip Roll is similar in most respects to a 360 Tip Roll. The only difference is that the spring is now so vigorous that all the weight is taken off the skis so the tips are lifted off the snow. Once lifted, the tips swing downhill past 360 and end up pointing down the fall-line. The mechanics are the same as the 360 Tip Roll. Remember to look in the direction of the twist, bring the boots in close to the hips, and push off the poles to complete the maneuver.

POLE FLIP

The Pole Flip is an aerial forward somersault using the poles to assist the initiation of the flip and for support in the air. The mechanics for the somersault are basically the same as a diving Forward Roll and a Front Flip. For best results use a ski a little shorter than your normal length so the tails will not get caught on the snow during the landing. Wear low-back boots or loose high-back boots, so that excessive knee strain will be avoided if the tails of the skis catch.

DESCRIPTION

First a small bump must be built, or a hole dug, or a mogul found that is hard enough to stop the skis when skied into at slow speeds. Then ski into the "stop" at a slow speed in a crouched position. When the skis hit the "stop," spring forward while reaching out with the arms over the front of the skis. The poles are planted about two feet in front of the ski tips for support and the chin tucked to the chest. The shoulders are hunched to round the back, bringing the hips straight over the head. The ski boots are tucked close to the hips to somersault quickly and prepare for the landing. As the feet come over the head, there is a push on the poles to assist the completion of the flip, and you land on your feet.

LEARNING STEPS

1. Begin by reviewing a Forward Roll without skis or poles. Then try some Pole Flips on the grass using only poles (see page 18). Emphasize a two-footed takeoff and getting over the poles. Ask someone to grasp one of your forearms so you won't land on your head. The spotter should be careful of the ski poles when they come around. Keep the palms of the hands on the tops of the poles for maximum support and stability.

2. Review the same thing on the snow without skis. Then build a small bump or hole that will stop the skis. Pile loose snow in the landing area to cushion the

impact. Warm up by doing some Forward Rolls with skis on and "press-ups" into a Tip Stand.

3. Have a spotter stand next to the "stop" where your arm can be grasped. A spotter will prevent you from landing on your head or neck. Then ski slowly into the "stop" in a crouched position. Spring up and forward, planting the poles in front of the skis. Tuck the head and roll forward and in the air. Keeping your ski boots close to your hips will help you to land on your feet.

ERROR CORRECTION

1. Skiers frequently fail to stop their skis to help initiate the flip. The skis must stop before the extension. The flex of the ski provides some assistance for the spring forward and into the air. Make the "stop" firm.

2. During the spring, the hips must be lifted at least as high as the head. This facilitates flipping over when the head is tucked under immediately following the pole plant.

3. Keep pressure on the ski poles once

POLE FLIP

the flip has started to keep you in the air. Do not allow your arms to give in completely so the body collapses between the poles.

Pole Stunts allow you to get higher into the air. As a result, harder falls and more bruises are possible. Care must be taken to avoid unnecessary bumps. Sequential learning is important. The terrain should be properly prepared and spotters should be used. The stunts are hard, but exciting to watch and perform.

8
UPRIGHT AERIALS

Exciting and spectacular, Aerial Acrobatics provide breathtaking thrills for the spectators and performers. "Get Air! Go for it!" the crowd yells. The aerialist feels the eyes of the audience upon him.

Many times this is the turning point that separates the highly trained athlete from the "Go for broke" competitor. The trained athlete knows what he can do. He has practiced continually and is confident of his skill. The performance is smooth, graceful, and shows marked precision.

The "Go for broke" competitor yields to the pressure of the moment. Inadequate knowledge and lack of practice weakens this competitor, who bolsters his confidence by an "I'll show you!" attitude. Sometimes he pulls it off, many times he doesn't. Frequently an injury forces him to stop completely. This type of individual becomes a statistic that medical groups and ski areas use to point out the dangers of Aerial Acrobatics. Fortunately, strict qualification procedures keep this type of individual from attempting dangerous aerials in competition. Competitors must qualify stunts

they are going to use in contests. Then they must indicate what they plan to do in competition by filing a "flight plan" before the competition begins.

Some injuries will occur even with the best coaching and training environment; but the serious athlete will look for ways to minimize the chances of injury. If aerial acrobats will take to heart the values of safety, understanding, and practice, they can stay healthy to jump again another day.

Before starting to learn aerials, skiers should become experts in selecting the safest location for building jumps and then they should learn how to build the correct takeoff to assist proper execution of the maneuver. Without learning these basic skills, they increase the possibilities of injury to themselves and others.

JUMP BUILDING
There are four major areas of concern in jump building: placement and size of the jump, preparing the jumping area, formation of the lips (takeoffs), and supervision during practice. All are extremely

TYPES OF JUMPS

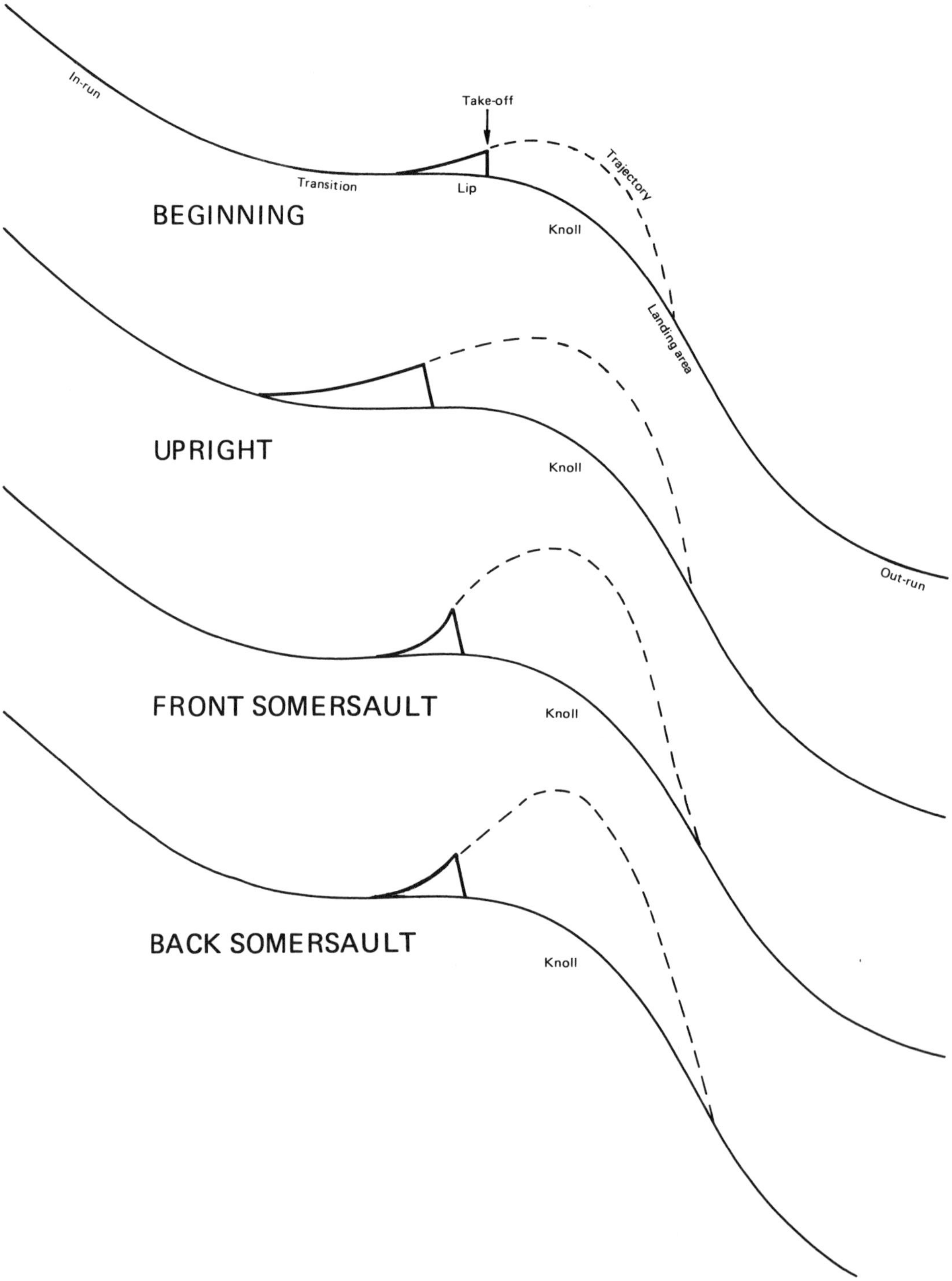

In-run

Take-off

Transition

Lip

Trajectory

BEGINNING

Knoll

Landing area

UPRIGHT

Knoll

Out-run

FRONT SOMERSAULT

Knoll

BACK SOMERSAULT

Knoll

important for safe practice. Each recommended procedure should be carefully studied.

PLACEMENT OF THE JUMP

Safety for the performer and spectators determines where and how a jump is built. The jump should be built on a knoll or roll with a smooth inrun, a steep hill to land on, and a long smooth outrun. This type of hill allows a jumper's trajectory (flight path) to follow the general shape of the terrain for maximum "air time" while limiting the height from which to fall. In many areas where contests have been scheduled, bulldozers have been used to build the appropriate type of terrain if one wasn't already available.

Exact placement of the takeoff on the knoll is influenced by many factors. Beginning jumpers may sail off a two-foot lip that is built right on the edge of the knoll. Experts may build larger jumps farther back from the edge (see illustration). Both are correctly trying to land on a steep surface to reduce their impact. Speed influences how far the jump is moved back from the landing area. The greater the speed, the farther the jumper will travel in the air and the farther the jump must be moved back from the landing. Other factors that influence placement of the jump are the height of the takeoff and the angle of the lip. All of these variables must be in balance for the jumper to land safely on the steep landing area.

The jump area should also be roped off and/or placed so passing skiers will not ski into the jumping area. High speeds and sometimes off-balanced positions of a jumper make the landing area and the long outrun particularly dangerous places. Care must be taken to ensure the safety of everyone in these two areas. Jumpers should make it their responsibility to keep these areas cleared and well groomed.

PREPARING THE JUMPING AREA

The ideal jumping hill should have a smooth, well-packed inrun. The longer the inrun, the greater the speed of the jumper and the farther the distance he will travel in the air. Both sides of the inrun should be packed out four or five ski lengths so the jumper can easily turn out if he doesn't want to complete his takeoff. The occasional wandering skier who ends up in the middle of the landing area or outrun makes this a necessity. If unpacked snow is left immediately next to the inrun, it could hinder a jumper who wishes to turn out and send him over the jump off-balance. The loose snow could also trip a jumper, exposing him to possible injury from a fall. Grooming both sides of the inrun reduces some of the risks in jumping.

The transition area and takeoff (lip) should be completely smooth and packed solid. Hardening chemicals may be applied to the snow to preserve the shape of the takeoffs for a longer period of time, ensuring jump consistency for aerialists.

There are several methods of building jumps before the final lips are shaped. The easiest is to have a bulldozer push the snow up into a mound, and do the finish work with shovels. However, the majority of jumps are built completely with shovels. Generally two methods are used: the slanted-ski method and the block method. The slanted-ski method involves forming a corral with all the skis of the jumpers, and shoveling snow into the corral until a mound of sufficient size is built so that the finishing work can begin. The biggest difficulty with this method is forming a base large enough so that the jump won't collapse after repeated practice. For the block method, the snow must be packed down, cut into blocks, and tapered to sit one on top of another to form an igloo-like base. To finish the foundation, snow is thrown inside. There are several examples of a block jump in the photographs of this book.

The landing area should be steep—the steeper the landing area, the less the jumper will feel the impact of the landing. A steep landing provides a glancing impact, much like a thrown rock skipping across the water. Packing the landing area and then padding it with loose snow provides a soft cushion for a jumper to land on when working on new stunts. After repeated jumps, a hole will develop at the spot where most people are landing. This hole must be filled with extra snow to keep the landing area smooth. On cloudy days, some type of marker, either dye or tree boughs, can be spread in the landing area so the jumpers can easily distinguish the ground from their position high in the air.

A well-built outrun provides plenty of distance and room for the jumper to slow down and turn out after coming off the jump at a high rate of speed. Frequently, this is the area where casual observers are hit; unaware of the high speeds, off-balance positions, and dangers of loose skis, individuals may wander into the outrun and become an injury statistic. To avoid accidents, keep this area well patrolled.

FORMATION OF THE LIPS (TAKEOFFS)

The formation of the lip or contour of the jump should be guided by the type of stunt to be attempted. Analyze the illustrations on page 124. Uprights and some twisting aerials require a smooth takeoff with a shallow contour to enhance a balanced, upright position while leaving the jump. Inverted aerials are helped by a smooth takeoff with a severe contour. The severe banana-shaped lip will actually assist the jumper's rotation in the proper direction to complete the somersault. A takeoff of this type is commonly known as a "Kicker" since it kicks the skier high into the air. Consequently, it is very important that the shape of the takeoff should be formed with a definite goal in mind. If the aerialist understands the body mechanics involved in a stunt, he

can build a lip that will assist the desired body action or position.

It is imperative that jumpers develop a system to control, protect, and maintain the safest possible conditions during practice. People must be kept out of the landing area. Unqualified individuals should not be allowed to jump. The landing area must be continuously groomed. Spotters are needed to clear the jump and warn of dangers so that jumpers have enough time to turn out. Skis, poles, shovels, and other tools must be kept away from the jumping area. All these factors must be taken into consideration during a practice period. Jumpers can develop a rotational system to handle these tasks and work together to assure maximum safety conditions.

PREPARING YOURSELF FOR JUMPING

After the jump is built and you are ready for your first jump, check all your ski gear. Your bindings should be in adjustment and runaway straps removed. The speed and impact of a fall can cause a released ski to "windmill" and cause severe injury if it is still attached to your leg. Not using runaway straps presents another problem: the danger caused by runaway skis. This is another reason for maintaining a well-patrolled and roped-off jumping area. Ski stops may solve both these problems. Pole straps should also be removed for the same reasons, as a "windmilling" pole can cause a severe wound.

In Upright Aerials there are certain fundamental goals that are common in the first jump as well as the more complex jumps that follow. Balance on the inrun, off the lip, in the air, and on the landing is the key. Efficiency of movement and timing in the takeoff and in the air are signs of a graceful, smooth performer. Fear, fatigue, lack of understanding, and an improperly prepared jump can all detract from a smooth, effortless ride. The following analysis of the first jump will cover the key factors that are basic to most Upright Aerials.

THE FIRST JUMP

Usually the first jump takes place off a lip that is no more than two feet above the natural contour of the slope. The inrun is shortened and the jumper flies five to ten feet before landing. As confidence increases, the jumper starts from a position higher up the inrun, sailing farther off the jump before landing. Since excitement and pleasure increase after each successful attempt, a word of caution is in order for the overzealous: Quit while the jumps are short and successful. Instilling fear or destroying confidence by a hard fall will slow the learning process for several days. Remember that success breeds success. End practices with a wild desire to get back to jumping at the first possible chance.

Before jumping again, check all of your gear. Remove your runaway straps and pole straps. Hike up the inrun to a point from which you would like to start and then step down the hill a few feet. Start from there. You will be more confident.

DESCRIPTION

For the first jump, the skier steps into a wedge position on the inside edges and faces down the inrun. The poles are planted in the snow to maintain a stationary position. To start down the inrun, the poles are lifted and the edges released by a lateral movement of the knees allowing the skis to run together parallel. The skier stands in a tall, relaxed flat-footed position. As the skis begin to climb the takeoff, the ankles and knees bend to compensate for the upward slope of the jump causing increased pressure on the balls of the feet. (The hands stay within peripheral vision and are carried in such a manner as to aid balance.) Just before the feet leave the

jump, there is a slight push off the balls of the feet straight up into the air. This is straight up in relation to the pull of gravity, not in relation to the angle of the jump. Pushing or jumping forward or rocking back will result in an off-balance position in the air. Once airborne, look for the landing spot. This helps maintain a balanced position by keeping the head in an upright position. During the flight, the knees are bent slightly by pulling the ski boots up under the hips. To prepare for the landing, the body is extended into a tall relaxed position with the hands and arms out to the side to aid balance upon impact. Upon impact, the joints of the body bend to absorb some of the force of the landing.

LEARNING STEPS

1. Mentally review the key factors of an Upright Aerial: (a) make a balanced inrun; (b) crouch to prepare for the spring; (c) spring straight up into the air off the balls of the feet; (d) sight the landing; (e) approach the landing extended; and (f) give in to the impact by bending at the body joints.
2. Begin practice on a very small jump that causes absolutely no fear. Gradually work up to larger jumps.
3. After several jumps, balance and control should be improving to the point that you can start learning stunts in the air. All Upright Aerials, no matter what stunts are attempted, are initiated in the same manner as the first jump. The only additional movement is performing the stunt once you are in the air—and not before. Thus, all Upright Aerials are just a matter of manipulating the position of the legs and counterbalancing with the upper body.

ERROR CORRECTION

1. Most beginners land on the tail of their skis during first attempts, because they leave the takeoff with more pressure on the heels of their feet. Fear usually causes people to slow down just before

THE
FIRST
JUMP

jumping, so they do a wedge that places them back on their heels just before takeoff. Remember that a correct Upright requires springing straight up off the balls of the feet. Start from a lower position on the inrun if you feel any fear.

2. Another common error is dropping the hands behind the body during flight. The hands should be kept in the field of vision during the spring and flight. The hands are excellent indicators of an off-balance position. For example, circling the arms in the air is a natural reaction to correct an off-balance position. A rapid circling will cause the body to rotate slowly on the lateral or somersaulting axis. It can correct a slightly off-balance position, given enough time in the air (see Appendix).

3. Frequently a beginner will spring off a jump leading with the chest while the head remains back. Remember to lead with the head. The jumper's body must rotate forward very slowly in the air to adjust for the differences in angles between the takeoff and the landing area. The body must be perpendicular to the landing slope upon touchdown. Since the body was at one angle on takeoff, it must be rotated forward to compensate for the new angle of the landing surface. Getting the head out forward will help to accomplish this movement.

GELÄNDE TUCK

The Gelände is a very balanced aerial maneuver that is used by experienced aerialists when jumping long distances. Jumps of over 200 feet have been done in the Gelände position.

DESCRIPTION
Simplest of the Upright Aerials, the Gelände requires little more than drawing the feet up underneath the hips once in the air. The drawing-up motion causes the knees to rise toward the chest and the ski tips to drop slightly. Hold this position for a moment, and then extend the legs for the landing.

LEARNING STEPS
1. This stunt (and all the others discussed here) can be practiced by doing the exercises listed under "Accelerate Learning Safely" beginning on page 18.
2. When standing on the hill, practice drawing one foot up underneath the hips while remaining upright.

3. Remember, the key points of the stunt are: (a) springing straight up off the lip of the jump; (b) looking for your landing spot—these first two points become habit with practice; (c) pulling the feet up under the hips and holding this position; and (d) extending for the landing.

ERROR CORRECTION

1. Most errors that occur in this stunt are typical of the errors found in all Upright maneuvers. If difficulty occurs in practice, go back to the section on the First Jump and review the fundamentals of balance, timing, and efficiency of movement. This suggestion applies to all Upright aerials.

2. Typically, beginners ride off the jump without springing. Generally they remain reasonably balanced, but they lack the spring that is needed to increase height and distance. Start from a lower spot on the inrun and work on the spring.

SPREAD
(Eagle)

This stunt is a popular long-distance high flyer, which provides a maximum of control in the air and is also the first

SPREAD

GELÄNDE TUCK

jump in which the arms are used to create a visual effect.

DESCRIPTION

After leaving the jump, the arms and legs spread out to the side and away from the body, much like the spokes of a wheel. This position is held until just before landing. Then the skis come together and the arms are drawn in closer to prepare for impact.

LEARNING STEPS

1. Review lead-up exercises for aerials.
2. Without skis on, jump into the air and practice the Spread position.
3. Then with skis on, practice one-half the movement by standing on one foot and spreading the other out to the side.

ERROR CORRECTION

1. Many inexperienced jumpers try the Spread right off the lip of the jump and end up off-balance in the air. Any foot push other than straight up will tend to set the hips spinning or twisting. If this isn't intentional, watch out! In all Upright Aerials, look for the landing spot first. After spotting the landing, perform the maneuver.
2. Another exercise to develop the feeling of going up in the air before doing the maneuver is to count out loud to three before doing the maneuver. This will help correct an early initiation.

TIP DROP

A Gelände is an excellent lead-up maneuver for the Tip Drop because the ski tips begin to drop when the feet are pulled up under the hips.

DESCRIPTION

After springing into the air, the knees are drawn up forward as they bend. At the same time, the heels of the ski boots are pulled up under the hips, causing the tips to drop at an angle of 45 degrees or more. This position is held until the body begins to extend to prepare for the landing.

LEARNING STEPS

1. Review the lead-up exercises for Upright Aerials. Without skis on, practice jumping into the air and holding the Tip Drop position briefly.
2. Practice Geländes by raising the heels of the boots closer to the hips while keeping the back straight.
3. Practice body placement while standing over a bump on one leg. This will allow the tip to drop freely into the correct position.

ERROR CORRECTION

1. Again, the most common and disastrous error is initiating the Tip Drop position from the edge of the jump. Wait until you are in the air for all Upright Aerials before changing body position.
2. Avoid bending the upper body forward at the waist. The back should remain straight and perpendicular to the general slope of the terrain.

TIP CROSS

A Tip Cross is a variation of the Tip Drop in that the ski tips drop down at a 45-degree angle while the skis cross. It may resemble a knock-kneed beginner caught with his skis crossed while trying to wedge.

DESCRIPTION

After leaving the jump the knees are bent and held together while the ski boots are pulled up under the hips. The feet are spread apart with the toes pulled inward and the heels pushed apart to cause the ski tips to cross. This position is held until the body begins to prepare for the landing.

LEARNING STEPS

1. Review the Tip Cross in a stationary position. Emphasize raising one ski and boot higher than the other so the skis can be easily crossed without catching or hanging up on each other.
2. Practice the stunt off a jump that allows plenty of "air time" so the skis can

be crossed and uncrossed without unnecessary rush.

1. Avoid bending forward at the waist. The back should remain straight and the hands and head up to maintain a vertical position in the air.

2. Do not attempt this maneuver off too small a jump, for it forces you to hurry the cross. Errors occur more often when people are rushed.

3. If the skis keep catching on each other, one ski boot should be raised high enough so it can be placed on the top of the lower boot, allowing several inches of clearance to cross the skis.

BACK SCRATCHER

A Back Scratcher is an exaggerated Tip Drop in which the skis point almost straight down at the snow as the tails touch the skier's back. The stunt requires an understanding of action-reaction balancing in the air (see Appendix).

DESCRIPTION

After "getting air," and not before, the feet push back as far as possible while the knees bend. The hips push forward, helping the ski tips to point straight down. The upper body leans back as the arms move behind the body to counter balance the action of the legs. This position is held for a moment and then the skis and arms come forward.

LEARNING STEPS

1. Review the lead-up exercises for Upright Aerials.

2. Practice Tip Drops but eliminate drawing the knees up and forward to drop the tips. Start pushing the feet back to bend the knees.

3. As the feet move back, allow the body to lean back naturally for balance in the air. Keep the hands high to maintain the upright position.

ERROR CORRECTION

1. Again, beginners frequently bend at the waist or knees. Keep your body straight all the way down to the knees. The back can arch slightly to counterbalance for the feet moving back.

2. Caution: First leave the jump with a straight-up spring. Then, and only then, push the feet back. Pushing the feet back too soon may result in a 30-foot nose-dive.

SIDE KICK
(Kick Out)

The Side Kick is a variation of the Tip Drop with a little twisting of the legs added.

DESCRIPTION

Once in the air the knees are bent as both legs begin turning to the side, pivoting at the hip joint. This causes the tips to drop at a 45-degree angle or more while the skis twist out sideways to about a 45-degree angle. The boots remain near or under the hips while the back is straight and the hands held high.

LEARNING STEPS

1. Practice lifting one ski and turning it to the side while in a stationary position. Develop a feel for turning the legs without turning the upper body.

2. Review a Tip Cross and concentrate on the actions of one leg.

3. Try the whole maneuver. Remember to keep the boots near or under the hips while the legs pivot at the hip.

ERROR CORRECTION

1. If the boots are kicked too far out to the side, the body will tilt sideways at the waist to counterbalance the movement of the feet. Do not correct this error because it is an excellent lead-up for a Mule Kick.

2. Avoid bringing the knees up too far—it draws the feet forward, causing a bend at the waist to maintain balance. The tips should drop approximately 45

TIP CROSS

BACK SCRATCHER

SIDE KICK

MULE KICK

degrees while the skis are twisted sideways at approximately 45 degrees.

MULE KICK

The Mule Kick is a 90 Degree Tip Drop with the legs turned out to the side at 90 degrees. Like the Back Scratcher, it requires a definite movement of the upper body to counterbalance the positioning of the lower body.

DESCRIPTION

After leaving the takeoff, the knees bend to a 90-degree angle as the feet push back. Both legs begin turning simultaneously to the side while pivoting at the hip joint. The head turns to look over the shoulder for the tails of the skis. The upper body tilts toward the tails of the skis and the arms raise to complete the balancing act. This position is held for a moment and then the body begins to extend for the landing.

LEARNING STEPS

1. Practice this position without skis. Balance on one leg while raising the other out to the side. Emphasize looking over your shoulder for the heel of the raised foot.
2. Review the same position with one ski on. Emphasize tilting your upper body toward the tails of the skis.
3. Try it on a jump that will give you enough time in the air. Remember to leave the jump and spot the landing before initiating the stunt. Think of pushing the skis out to the side and then hanging out a car window to look at them.

ERROR CORRECTION

1. Frequently jumpers land with their skis at an angle to the outrun. This quarter twist is either caused by initiating the maneuver on the lip of the jump or forgetting to tilt the upper body sideways toward the skis.
2. If balance is a problem, keep your arms high above your body, and try to place your head over the ski boots to encourage tilting the upper body to counterbalance for the action of the legs.

DAFFY

The Daffy looks scary, is scary, and yet is easy to do. It is a high flyer that can really eat up the distance. The Daffy is similar to the Spread because the arms and legs again spread, except one leg goes forward and the other goes back. Putting two or more of these together constitutes a Space Walk.

DESCRIPTION

After leaving the jump, the front leg is raised high and forward with the knee straight. The back leg trails and bends slightly at the knee in order for the tip of the trailing ski to point straight down. The position resembles the "splits" in the air. The arms are extended to the side for balance (or one is held forward and the other is held back to counterbalance for the actions of the legs). The legs are brought together under the hips before landing.

LEARNING STEPS

1. If you lack the flexibility to do the "splits," then start stretching exercises. It may take several months to loosen up your leg muscles so you can do this stunt. If you are not capable of doing the splits and still want to do the Daffy, you will have to bend the back leg and lean slightly forward at the waist to compensate for the raised front leg.
2. Practice kicking your front leg forward in a stationary position. Bend forward at the waist to remain balanced.
3. Use a jump that gives plenty of "air time." Start by kicking the leg up just a little at first, working it to a higher position as your balance improves.

ERROR CORRECTION

1. An early initiation will cause you to twist off the jump. Spring into the air before raising the legs. Considerable ab-

DAFFY

dominal strength is required to raise that front leg high.

2. The front knee should not be bent. Concentrate to keep it straight.

3. If the hips are allowed to turn to the side during initiation, the body will twist in the air. The head and hips should face straight ahead during the kickup to position.

The maneuvers just discussed are the basics. Many of these stunts can be done in combination with other stunts. The ingenuity of the combinations is limited only by the creativity of the competitor and his understanding of the mechanics.

Remember, in Upright Aerials, the jump should be built to facilitate a balanced straight-up takeoff. Then the stunts are done in the air after leaving the jump.

9

INVERTED
AERIALS

Somersaulting with skis has mushroomed in the last few years. Previously, somersaulting off a ski jump was considered foolhardy as very few skiers had the courage or skill necessary to attempt somersaults. Those experts who could somersault received tremendous attention wherever they traveled. But all of that has changed today with many skiers doing front and back somersaults. This change was brought about by an increased awareness of the mechanics of somersaulting due to the rapid transfer of gymnastic and springboard diving knowledge to the ski hill. Many gymnasts and divers became skiers and began experimenting with somersaults off bumps into soft snow. Now jumpers are holding hands and somersaulting. A few are doing multiple somersaults, some with twists.

Still, attempting a somersault off a jump should be approached with extreme caution. Inverted Aerials increase the possibility of landing on one's head or neck, and falls of this nature can result in severe injuries. Somersaults should *not* be attempted until the aerialist can perform all of the lead-up stunts as well as understand the mechanics and safety procedures.

The use of modern teaching equipment can greatly aid the learning process. Tumbling mats, diving boards, or trampolines should be used to master somersaults before attempts are made on snow. Artificial ski jumps with water or mats for a landing are especially beneficial. Properly taught, with a multitude of previous somersaulting experiences, a well-trained student should be able to experience success on his first jump attempt. Injuries should be almost nonexistent if the skier has been taught how to protect his head, neck, and extremities in a fall.

GENERAL PRINCIPLES
OF SOMERSAULTING

Skiers must learn how to initiate and complete a somersault before attempting it on skis. Without this prior training, attempting a somersault is foolhardy. The subtleties involved in initiating and controlling somersaults are rarely seen by an untrained observer.

FRONT SOMERSAULT IN PIKE POSITION

Center of gravity

Line of vision

INITIATING FRONT SOMERSAULTS

To initiate a Front Somersault off a jump, the body leans forward, moving the center of gravity in front of the feet (see Appendix). The feet push against the takeoff by an extension of the legs, resulting in a further movement forward of the center of gravity. The leg extension pushes the hips up as the upper body continues to bend forward at the waist, causing the body to spin around its center of gravity. It is important to remember that the head and shoulders must lead the body into the somersault, and the feet must provide the push against the jump to initiate the spin around the center of gravity, for once in the air you have all the spin you will ever have. (It is possible to create an extremely slow somersaulting action in the air by spinning the arms rapidly; however, this method of somersaulting is neither practical nor efficient.) A spin can be speeded up by tucking the body into a tight ball, but a faster spin in the "layout" position cannot be created once you are in the air. Therefore, the initiation of the somersault must begin on the ski jump. In order to more fully understand what can and cannot be done in the air, we recommend careful study of the Appendix.

INITIATING BACK SOMERSAULTS

The same principles apply for initiating Back Somersaults. The upper body bends backward by arching the back. The backward bend moves the center of gravity behind the feet, then a push off the balls of the feet against the jump causes an up and backward movement of the center of gravity. The initial forward momentum caused by skiing down the inrun still throws the body up and forward into the air, but the action of the spin itself, irrespective of the forward movement caused by skiing, does not change (see Appendix). The body still arches back and pushes off the balls of the feet. The leg extension pushes the hips up as the

BACK SOMERSAULT IN TUCK POSITION

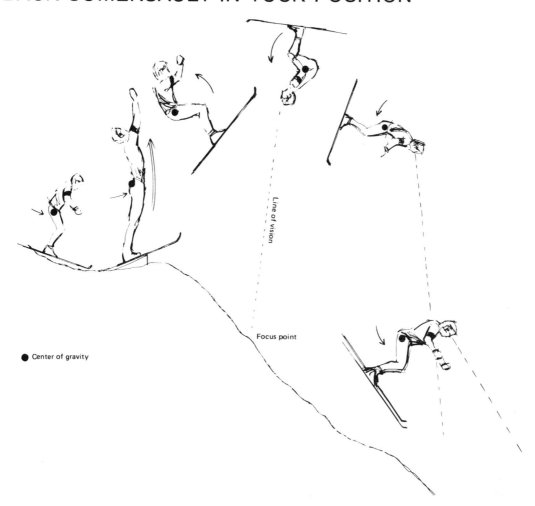

Line of vision

Focus point

● Center of gravity

upper body continues to arch back, causing the body to spin around its center of gravity. It is important to reemphasize that initiation occurs on the jump—for if the aerialist does not push off the jump to initiate the spin, he will become "stuck" in the air because Newton's action-reaction law takes effect. For example, the head and arms are dropped down, the legs will rise up to the body to counteract this movement, resulting in a "cannonball" position. Unless the legs can push against something to initiate the rotation, a somersault will not occur. Clearly, for all somersaulting jumps, the body must begin rotating around its center of gravity before the skis leave the ramp.

INITIATING SIDE SOMERSAULTS

To initiate a Side Somersault the hips must be tilting upward and to the side as the upper body begins to rotate in the direction of the spin. Beginning with the weight on the balls of the feet to compensate for the slant of the lip, there is a strong push off the outside foot to create a tipping of the head, shoulders, and hips in the direction of the somersault. Thus, on takeoff, the body is in a side-arch position with no lean forward or back. The chest faces down the hill during the entire maneuver. Any twisting movement on the lip will cause a loss of balance in the air. The landing is seen during the whole somersault. The push off the outside foot is a key element in

SIDE SOMERSAULT IN TUCK POSITION

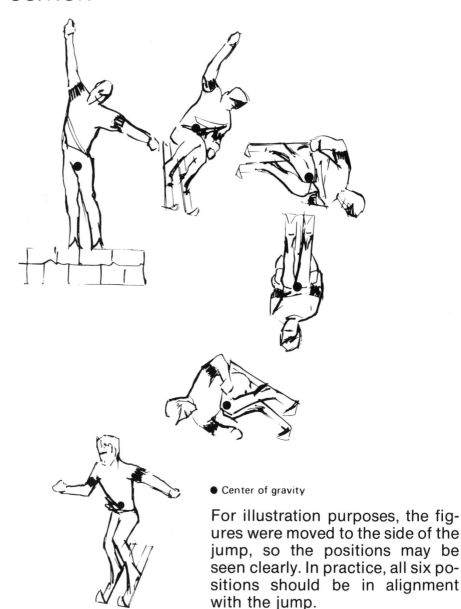

● Center of gravity

For illustration purposes, the figures were moved to the side of the jump, so the positions may be seen clearly. In practice, all six positions should be in alignment with the jump.

the maneuver since the contour of the lip does very little to assist the rotation of the Side Somersault.

CHANGING THE SPEED OF THE SOMERSAULT

Although the force of the initiation cannot be increased once the aerialist leaves the jump, the speed of the spin can be altered by changing body positions (see Appendix). Basically, the body spins faster as it becomes more compact, so the closer the arms and legs are to the spinning axis, the faster the body will spin. An example of this is the aerialist who spins rapidly in the tuck and slowly in the layout position. But remember, any change of body position af-

POSITIONS FOR SOMERSAULTING

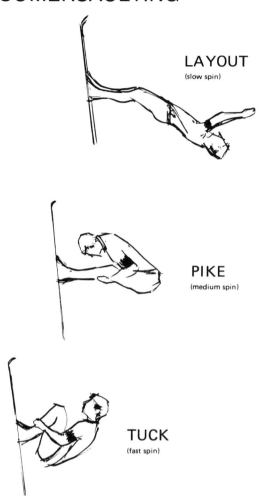

LAYOUT
(slow spin)

PIKE
(medium spin)

TUCK
(fast spin)

fects the speed of the spin. A straight body position (layout) with the arms extended over the head has the greatest inertia (see Appendix) and, consequently, is the slowest possible way to somersault. Bringing the arms to the side shortens the length of the body from the extended position, so a faster spin results. Arching the back also brings the head and feet closer to the spin axis, so this position is slightly faster than a straight body position. The pike position, characterized by straight legs and bending at the hips, is even faster. A complete tuck with head between the knees is the fastest possible spinning position.

It is important to note that a spin or twist can never be completely stopped. Once it has been initiated, a spin can be slowed only by lengthening the body into an open pike or layout position. This device is commonly used by divers and gymnasts who spin rapidly in a tuck position and then begin to lengthen their body to a pike or layout position before they become vertical to the landing surface. Careful observation will confirm that although the spinning is greatly reduced, it is not entirely stopped.

SAVING SOMERSAULTS

The importance of understanding how to change the speed of a somersault takes on greater meaning when there exists a possibility of a crash because the original spin was too fast or too slow. A short somersault is one in which there is not enough spin. An aerialist who realizes (either by kinesthetic feel or use of a focus point) that he will underspin his somersault can speed up his rotation by becoming more compact (bringing his body closer to the spin axis). In Front Somersaults, most aerialists tuck quickly to speed up the spin. In Reverse Somersaults, piking from a layout position usually gives enough added spin to complete a short somersault.

If a jumper has developed too much spin, he can slow down the speed of rotation by lengthening his body. He can extend his arms overhead to make himself as tall as possible and eliminate the back arch. Many times this can be seen when an aerialist has more air than he anticipated. He comes out of his tuck much sooner, and stretches to his full length with his arms and poles overhead to slow the spin down.

BASIC POSITIONS FOR SOMERSAULTING

Once a somersault is initiated on a jump, controlling the speed of spin and beauty of execution depends upon an understanding of the positions aerialists may use to complete a somersault as well as their personal body build. Individuals vary physically in many different ways. The length and breadth of their body and extremities and location of the center of gravity can alter the speed at which they spin. Also the position they use when somersaulting has its own unique characteristics.

In determining what position to use when selecting a stunt, the following questions should be carefully evaluated:

(1) What are the requirements of the stunt? Multiple somersaults require a faster spin. Spinning is more rapid in a tuck position than in a layout position.

(2) What is the distance to be covered in the air? Single somersaults, over a greater distance, allow for the more graceful, slower-spinning somersaults in the layout position.

(3) What positions do you prefer to use when practicing on the diving board or trampoline? Different body types will adapt to the various flipping positions differently.

(4) Is visibility a problem in the landing area? Cloudy days reduce the sharp contrast of the snow, impairing the depth perception of the aerialist. A very small, quick flip may be desirable in this situation.

Analyze the following positions in terms of speed of spin, degree of difficulty, and beauty:

Tuck: The tuck is the fastest spinning position. In the tuck position, the jumper is wrapped into a tight ball, the knees are bent, separated, and pulled in close to the chest. The upper body is bent forward and the hands grasp the shins just below the knees, helping to pull the legs closer to the chest.

A spread-knee tuck is recommended for several reasons. This position provides the fastest possible spin because the aerialist can ball-up tighter, decreasing the moment of inertia about the

SPREAD-KNEE TUCK POSITION

spin axis. For this reason, many aerialists attempting double and triple somersaults are now using this tighter position. Also, with the head tucked between the knees, the chances of head or neck injury are reduced. The jawbone won't crash against the top of the knees if the performer falls in this position.

Pike: Although the pike position is not commonly used in jumping competition, a brief analysis is included because of its value in changing the speed of a spin gracefully when correcting body position before landing impact. The pike position can be performed two different ways. In both methods, the aerialist is bent at the waist and the legs are held straight.

In the closed-pike position, the body is bent at the waist with the legs remaining straight. The arms grasp the legs just behind the knees. The upper body is pulled close to the thighs. For Forward Spins, the head is down but positioned so the jumper is able to see over or between his legs. For Reverse Somersaults, the head is raised.

In the open-pike position, the arms are extended to the side at right angles to the body. This position is very attractive, but difficult to maintain because it requires the aerialist to keep the abdominal and thigh muscles tightly contracted during the spin.

The advantage of learning the open pike is that it can be used to slow down the spin from a tuck somersault by extending the legs to a straight position. It can also be used to increase the rate of spinning from a layout position by bending at the waist, allowing the legs to come in closer to the body.

Layout: The layout position is commonly used in Reverse Somersaults because of its grace and beauty. It is a slow-spinning position that is difficult to control because the slightest tilt of the body sideways will begin a slow-twisting action (see Appendix). Also, the speed of spin must be timed perfectly to avoid bending at the knees or waist, which eliminates the layout position. In the layout position, the body and legs are straight or slightly arched and the arms are extended to the side at right angles to the body.

Because of the extreme difficulty of controlling the amount of spin from a jump, a complete somersault done in a layout position is rarely seen. Rather, most competitors will combine the layout with a quick pike or tuck at the end of the somersault to control for the landing. It is a rare circumstance when a competitor completes the whole somersault without breaking at the waist in order to make a last-second adjustment before landing.

Sometimes a layout position is used when the aerialist senses that he has too much spin in the pike or tuck. Then he will open into a layout position much sooner, stretching out to his fullest length, in order to slow the speed of the spin and adjust for the landing.

Occasionally an aerialist will start to spin in a layout position until a half turn has been completed. Then the body is quickly bent into a pike or tuck position to complete the somersault. This is called a Flying or Delayed Somersault. It is performed with Front and Back Somersaults.

SETTING A FOCUS POINT

As aerialists become more proficient, they often develop a "feel" as to where they are in the air. Through constant practice and evaluation, they learn to use the length of the inrun, the force of initiation, and the steepness of the landing area to determine where and when they are going to extend to slow the spin for the landing.

However, it is possible and advisable to use a focus point to determine relative position in the air in relation to the surroundings. A focus point is a spot, point, or object in the environment that is previously selected by the performer to be used as a gauge to establish body position when performing Ballet or Aerial maneuvers. Aerialists doing Back Somersaults almost naturally select the landing area for a focus point since they can see it long before they land.

In stunts with blind landings (the landing is not seen until just before the time of impact), consistent performers make use of their vision to cue on an object. Visual cues (focus points) are an integral part of a Front Somersault, Front Moebius, and multiple somersaults. Competitors may select the horizon line, the tree line, the banner on the jump, or some permanent fixture that is easy to locate for a focus point. Jumpers should train themselves to do this whenever possible since it is one more factor that takes the guesswork out of some potentially difficult and dangerous stunts.

COMING OUT

The function of the focus point is to determine when an aerialist should come out of a maneuver—that is, extending the body to slow the speed of rotation preparatory to landing. In a properly timed somersault, the body extends to pike or layout position before the body is perpendicular to the snow. If the extension that slows the speed of the somersault does not occur, the aerialist will either roll right over the front of his skis in a Front Somersault or fall over backwards in a Back Somersault when the skis shoot out from underneath his hips.

Coming out can be used only in a tuck or pike position, since the body may be extended from these positions to make final spin corrections before landing. In the layout position, the aerialist can't make use of this skill to assure the correct amount of spin. For this reason, complete layout maneuvers are rarely seen since they allow very little opportunity for spin adjustments in the air. Rather, most aerialists throw a short layout and accelerate to the coming-out point with a quick pike or tuck.

METHODS OF SPOTTING

Most athletes who have had any association with aerial stunts are familiar with methods used by coaches to help an individual through a stunt. The number of different methods for assisting or spotting inverted aerials is quite limited because of the difficulty of keeping contact with the skier, who moves quite a distance in any aerial stunt. However, voice cues and hand assists can be used.

Voice Cues: Voice cues are usually limited to one word reminders. The spotter and the jumper work together to determine the meaning of the command and when it is to be used. In the Reverse Somersault, using the term "Hips!," shouted just at the time the jumper should start moving the hips forward, will help remind him of a key movement. It is also an aid in learning timing of the initiation. "Now!" could be used to call a skier out of a Front Double Somersault so he will land on his feet. "Look!" could remind the skier to look for the focus point to determine where he is in the air. The important thing is to associate the word with the action and practice the association *before* jumping. Then, just hearing the noise will cause the jumper to react because he has been preconditioned to respond to the command. Voice commands develop a keen sense of concentration on the key factors of the stunt.

Hand Spotting During Initiation: Hand spotting during the initiation of a somersault can be done from a platform built near the top of the lip and to either side. The spotter stands on the platform and assists the initiation of the somersault to assure a strong initiation. For Front Somersaults, the spotter places his hand on the jumper's boots or lower legs and pushes them up and back in the direction of the spin. For Back Somersaults,

HAND SPOTTING: INITIATION AND LANDING

the spotter must be very quick to push on the back of the jumper's lower legs to assist forward rotation in the direction of the spin. This method of spotting will not guarantee a perfect landing. However, it is an effective spotting technique for assisting the initiation of a somersault while exposing the spotter to very little danger.

Hand Spotting in the Landing Area: Hand spotting in the landing area is considerably more complicated and exposes the spotter to possible injury. In this method, the spotter and the jumper determine where to start on the inrun so the jumper will land in approximately the same spot on each jump. Then the take-off is marked, sometimes with dye, so all jumpers start their initiation at the same place and in the same direction. The spotter then places himself about five to eight feet up the hill from the spot where the jumper lands. He stands just to the side, almost in the jumper's intended flight path. From this position, he is capable of placing his hand on the jumper's chest or back to assist him over if he is short in his spin. The danger for the spotter is obvious. He has to know what he is doing and he has to have confidence that his skier will jump in the intended direction. The advantage of this method of assistance is that it assures the skier will not land on his head. He will

at least make it to his shoulders or back. In the Reverse Somersault, the hand is placed under the body and on the chest to provide a lifting spinning action to help complete the somersault. Skiers doing Front Somersaults can be assisted by a hand being placed under the body and on the back to help the spin and lift. Although this method is rarely seen, it is extremely effective. We caution, however, that these methods of assisting a jumper should only be attempted by spotters or coaches who are extremely competent and have experience spotting in gymnastics.

Elevated Landing Area: Another method of spotting and reducing the impact caused by falling is to jump onto an elevated landing area. Spotters can stand in the landing area at a point where the student can be assisted to complete the rotation. This method allows the spotter to keep eye contact with the skier so voice cues can be used at any time. It also emphasizes the importance of an upward extension to initiate somersaults. The landing area should be padded with loosely packed snow. When skiers have mastered the initiation, the landing area should be cut down or the jumpers should move to another jump with a steep fall-away landing area.

Analyze new methods of spotting as they develop. The function of spotting is

to provide maximum protection to the participants, both the performer and spotter. Skiers should not be led to believe that they are doing everything correctly until they can repeat the correct movements unassisted many times over. If a skier believes he is somersaulting even though the spotter is providing key assistance, he may try a somersault on his own with disastrous results. Be honest. Sometimes we are overambitious and end up injuring ourselves. Try to create the ideal safety situation for somersaulting. Although infrequently used, mouth guards and helmets also will provide added protection to the head.

PREPARING FOR A CRASH

Occasionally aerialists get "lost" in the air and lose their orientation or sense of direction. When this occurs, or when a jumper knows a crash is inevitable, every effort should be made to protect the head, neck, and extremities before impact. The body should fold into a spread-knee tucked position. The head and neck are least vulnerable when the chin is tucked to the chest and the shoulders are hunched to round the back. The knees are spread so the head can be tucked in between and the elbows and arms are held close to the body. In this rounded position, the body can absorb a considerable impact. This is an extremely important position to learn, particularly before learning Back Somersaults, where the chin is dangerously raised and the back is arched, exposing the body in a very vulnerable position. If the back remains arched, its flexibility is reduced. A severe impact could force the back beyond its range of flexibility, causing a tearing of muscles, tendons, ligaments, and even bones. We cannot stress strongly enough how important it is to learn to protect your body before attempting potentially dangerous stunts. Learn all the lead-up exercises and safety procedures before your first attempts.

FORMING A TAKE-OFF FOR SOMERSAULTS

A somersaulting jump should have all the general characteristics of any well-planned jump: smooth inrun, solid take-off, steep landing, and long outrun. (Illustration, page 124.) The only variable should be the shape or contour of the takeoff. Upright aerials require a takeoff that provides a balanced straight-up lift. Inverted aerials, on the other hand, require a takeoff that will assist the initiation of the somersault.

The lip of a somersault jump has a banana-shaped contour. It should be severe enough to cause the skis to increase reverse camber (flex) as they ride up the lip. Then, in conjunction with a push from the feet, the skis can unflex, snapping back to their original shape, causing a rebound that acts like a springboard to help "kick" the skier high into the air. Because of this action, these jumps are called "kickers."

Front Somersault Kicker: The Front Somersault Kicker is generally much steeper and more abrupt than the Back Somersault lip. The steep Front Somersault lip helps to initiate the somersault by slowing the skis as the head and upper body continue forward, moving the center of gravity ahead of the feet. The subsequent unflexing of the skis and push of the feet force the hips and heels upward, rotating behind the upper body for initiation of the somersaulting action. Sometimes instructors build lips so steep that the skis actually stop and the skier is "flipped" over the front of the lip. While this may be a good idea to help beginners somersault the first time, such a somersault is very difficult to control, and depends upon the snow's retaining enough hardness so it won't break under the pressure of the "jammed" skis.

Back Somersault Kicker: The "kicker" for a Back Somersault is less severe than for a Front Somersault. The key to a Back Somersault is to push off the balls of the feet, pushing the hips forward and arching the back. If a lip is too severe, it is difficult to remain balanced and initiate the somersault correctly. The back "kicker" with a severe lip has a tendency to set the aerialist back on his heels. Yet a slight "kick" is desirable to attain greater height in the air to improve the overall look of a maneuver.

The guidelines just presented on jump building are by no means the only ways a jump can be built. Among some Freestylers, there is considerable controversy over the ideal shapes for a takeoff. Through experience you will develop a preference for a particular shape for the various maneuvers. Then you should always try to approximate that shape when building or selecting a lip for jumping.

Inverted Aerials require a high degree of training. Therefore, Upright Aerials and *all* lead-up exercises should be mastered so a comfortable feeling for somersaulting develops. Bypassing or short-cutting any of these steps increases the chances of injury. Study the key movements and practice in safe conditions so you can jump again another day.

FRONT SOMERSAULT

The Front Somersault is considered a blind stunt since the aerialist does not have sufficient time to view the landing area in order to make final spin corrections before impact. Accordingly, it is difficult to complete this maneuver in a balanced position. Aerialists must develop a fine sense of feel for this maneuver through repeated practice and use of their peripheral vision to determine when to come out.

Even though it is difficult to land in a balanced position after completing a Front Somersault, it is possible to ski out of most landings since the body is spinning in the direction of travel. An aerialist can land almost flat on his back and, as long as he holds his boots near his hips, can roll up to a standing position. Such an ending is thus similar to the ending of a Forward Roll or Layback. If a somersault is overspun, then tucking the head and allowing a Forward Roll to occur is much better than the abrupt smashing impact that occurs when the body is in the layout position. The Front Somersault also provides a high degree of protection for the head and spinal column. Placing the head between the knees allows the shoulders and knees to take the impact of a fall rather than the head and neck.

The Front Somersault can be done in the tuck, pike, or layout position. The layout position can be combined with either of the other positions to create a slow rotating somersault coupled with a quick spin. In each instance, the somersault is initiated in the same manner and the desired position is held in the air. Each position will be discussed briefly after the general description.

DESCRIPTION
To do a Front Somersault in a tuck position, look down the inrun and select a focus point that can be used to signal the coming out to slow the rotation of the somersault. Mentally review the exact motions of the somersault and landing.

When ready, push off with poles and drop them on the snow to the side. (Dropping the poles eliminates one more hazard that could cause an injury.) When approaching the transition, crouch slightly, putting more weight on the balls of the feet. The hands are brought slightly forward at chest height with the elbows pointing down, just outside the line of the body. When the feet are within a foot or two of the top of the lip, the somersault is initiated by springing up and forward over the fronts of the skis, pushing hard off the balls of the feet. At the same time, the hands and arms extend forward to assist the initiation. The center of gravity must be ahead of the feet at the moment of initiation. Immediately after the up-forward spring and extension of the body, the upper body bends down sharply at the waist. The

FRONT SOMERSAULT
IN TUCK POSITION

hands snap down to grasp the lower legs as the knees are bent and the head is tucked to the chest. Spin in this position until the focus point is spotted, or until you feel it is time to come out. To open out of the tuck position, the hands are released from the legs. As they straighten, look down at the landing area and get the feet just ahead of or under the hips a moment before impact. The impact of the landing is absorbed by bending at the ankles, knees, and hips.

LEARNING STEPS

1. Review the lead-up exercises for Front Somersaults. Emphasize leaning forward and extending off the balls of the feet to initiate the somersault. Do Forward Rolls, Diving Forward Rolls on the snow or mats, and somersaults off mini-trampolines and trampolines. Practice standing somersaults off the end of diving boards. Learn Forward Rolls, Pole Flips, and Shoulder Rolls with skis on. If a mini-trampoline is available, set it on the snow in such a way that you can jump down on the bed with your ski boots and somersault downhill onto a soft padded landing. Keep the bed dry or covered with a nonslippery surface. Have spotters positioned to the side to prevent landing on the mini-trampoline or overspinning. The mini-trampoline provides a good on-the-snow review of the Front Somersault just prior to your first attempts off the jump.

2. For first attempts, build the lip of the jump extremely steep and abrupt so the skis will almost stop when they hit the lip. Then the body will continue forward ahead of the skis, and the skis will provide a spring. Prepare the landing area with a cushion of soft snow.

3. Now work on feeling the lip with your skis. Slide up the lip so that your ski tips stop at the end of the lip. Feel your skis flex on the jump. At the moment when the skis stop, spring up and forward as if doing a Front Somersault. The tails of the skis should lift off the snow. If the action is strong enough you can actually tip over forewards. Have a spotter available to prevent your falling over the front of the lip. Have an experienced aerialist complete a Front Somersault off your jump. He can tell you where you should start on the inrun.

4. At your starting point on the inrun, select your focus point and review each step of the complete somersault in your mind. Imagine yourself successfully somersaulting and landing. When you

are ready, push off and drop your poles on the snow. Concentrate on pushing off the balls of the feet and leaning forward on the initiation. Keep the knees spread while somersaulting. Look for the focus point and extend when you see it. Absorb the landing to reduce the impact.

5. Immediately review the maneuver mentally after your first attempt. Analyze what your body did during the total maneuver. Did you cover the key points? Review again at the top of the inrun before your next attempt.

ERROR CORRECTION

1. The biggest error is failing to spring forward off the balls of the feet. Fear usually causes skiers to hesitate on the

FRONT SOMERSAULT IN PIKE POSITION

jump, and as a result they spring off the heels of their feet. Although it is scary, the body must be leaning forward when extending off the balls of the feet.

2. Avoid bringing your knees up to your chest. "Chase your legs" by moving your upper body toward the lower body to snap into the tuck position.

3. When in doubt, initiate the somersaulting action a little early. It will result in a low flying somersault, but you will get over. If you push too late, you will become "stuck" in the air.

4. "Jamming" the skis into the jump without springing upward can result in a very fast, uncontrolled somersault. The lip is supposed to slow the skis while the upper body springs ahead and up into the air.

5. Closing the eyes is usually a result of fear. Select a large focus point and really look for it. Concentrate on seeing that object while you spin.

6. Somersaulting off-balance or twisting is usually caused by pushing harder off one foot, by turning the head and shoulders, or by not bringing the hips directly over the head. Work toward an even takeoff with both sides of the body working as a unit.

7. Failing to remain standing after what looks like an excellent landing is usually caused by a failure to concentrate on the end of the stunt. Once the somersault is made, many skiers just relax because they are so happy they made it over. Remember to extend for a landing, absorb the impact, and resist a fall by increasing muscular tension to stop the absorbing or bending by the body.

8. Snapping to a tuck position before leaving the takeoff is a common error. The desire to survive instills a little fear in us, so there is a tendency to hurry everything along so we can make it over. Leaving the jump in a forward leaning tuck will initiate a slow, spinning somersault. Strive for an up-forward spring just before leaving the jump to facilitate greater height and spin.

FRONT SOMERSAULT IN PIKE POSITION

The Front Somersault in pike position is initiated in the same manner as the Front Somersault in tuck. The body leans forward ahead of the feet just before the up-forward extension off the balls of the feet. Immediately, the upper body bends

sharply at the waist with the head going down toward the knees. The hands snap down and grasp just behind the knees or upper legs. The knees remain straight after the extension and throughout the somersault. Once the focus point is spotted, the hands release the legs and the body unfolds and extends for a landing.

The pike position can be learned before attempting it on skis. The most difficult aspect of this position is keeping the knees straight. Most skiers know that falling with the knees straight increases the chances of injury to this joint, and so they tend to bend the knees slightly while somersaulting. The body also tends to unfold from this position if not held tightly by grasping behind the legs. The aerialist must concentrate on pulling his upper body into his lower body during the somersault to get the tightest possible pike, since this is a slower spinning position than a tuck.

FRONT SOMERSAULT IN LAYOUT POSITION

To attain a layout position in a Front Somersault, the feet or heels must be pushed up and back immediately after initiation to form an arched position. Many beginners mistakenly try to arch by throwing their arms out to the side and pushing out their chest. This action can stall the somersaulting action. The arch position is formed by a movement of the lower body upward and back in a circular fashion following the up-forward spring off the jump. The foot push on the jump just continues up into the air. Then the layout position is held during the remainder of the somersault, unless it becomes necessary to change the speed of the rotation to complete the somersault before impact. If the layout is held for the complete flip, the knees and hips should be slightly flexed, breaking the layout position, just before landing to absorb the shock.

Since spinning is slowest in the layout position and very difficult to control without breaking form, a complete layout somersault is rarely seen. Usually competitors use a layout position in conjunction with a pike or tuck at the end of the somersault giving them time to correct any twisting that may have occurred on initiation and to control the speed of their spin.

FRONT SOMERSAULT IN LAYOUT POSITION

BACK SOMERSAULT

A Back Somersault is not any harder to do than a Front Somersault. In fact, most aerialists who can do both with a high degree of skill prefer doing the Back Somersault because the landing area is visible long before impact, giving the aerialist plenty of time to make minor adjustments in the spin to ensure a balanced landing. Yet the learning process for a Back Somersault is more difficult than a Front Somersault and considerably more treacherous. Several factors account for the difficulty involved in learning this maneuver.

First of all, the stunt can be learned on trampolines and off diving boards with little danger, yet off a jump it is extremely difficult to spot a skier and prevent him from landing on his head.

Second, a certain amount of fear causes skiers to hesitate on first attempts. The hesitation creates a ten-dency to lean excessively backwards on the heels of the feet and bend the knees. The resulting improper initiation of the somersault can result in hitting the back of the head on the jump.

Third, the head, neck, and back do not receive the protection a Front Somersault tuck provides. The head is up and back instead of being tucked in between the knees. The back is straighter instead of rounded. Because of this position, the halfway landing that might result from panic, change of mind, or not enough rotational spin is considerably more dangerous than bouncing off the snow in the front tuck position.

And last, the spin during a Back Somersault is opposite to the direction of travel, reducing the margin for error in landings. The angle at which an aerialist can land and still remain standing in a Back Somersault is substantially less than the Front Somersault. If the aerialist doesn't open and slow his spin before landing, the spinning action will shoot

his skis ahead, resulting in a painful crash on the back or head.

All of the above is not designed to discourage you from learning the Back Somersault, but to make you aware of the importance of getting some capable help and to prevent your being foolish because you are unaware of the danger. Back Somersaults should be approached with caution and careful planning by every skier regardless of ability.

DESCRIPTION

Mentally review the exact movements of a Back Somersault in the tuck position while standing at the top of the inrun, visualizing the whole maneuver including the landing. On the inrun the body is slightly crouched with the head forward and the hips back, balancing on the whole foot. The arms and hands are behind the hips and a couple of inches away from the side of the body. As the skis climb the contour of the takeoff, the hands and hips begin moving forward

BACK SOMERSAULT
IN TUCK POSITION

and upward, increasing pressure on the balls of the feet as the upper body bends back. With a complete extension of the legs, the somersault is initiated by a spring off the balls of the feet and a push of the hips up and forward while the upper body continues to bend back. The arms lift up for height. The head follows the motion of the arms, looking up and back. The speed of the somersaulting action is increased by bringing the knees up to the hands to form a tuck position. The head continues to look back for the landing area or a focus point. Upon spotting the landing area, the body begins to open up by releasing the hands and extending the legs to slow the spin and land.

LEARNING STEPS

1. Learn how to do a Back Somersault in gymnastics or diving to help prepare you for your first attempt on skis. Practice under supervision and coaching until you are confident. Remember the key points are to push off the balls of the

feet, bend back with the upper body, reach upwards with the arms, bringing the knees up to the hands to form a tuck position, and look for the landing area.
2. Just as in the Front Somersault, the shape of the lip plays an important part in the completion of the Back Somersault. The angle of the lip to the landing area is such that only two-thirds of a somersault is needed for a successful landing. Also, the slant of the lip will automatically place the hips in front of the heels and upper body if you remain perpendicular to your skis as they rise off the lip. The combination of these things takes much of the work out of executing a Back Somersault.
3. Watch more experienced jumpers complete Back Somersaults. Picture yourself on their skis and imagine what it is like. Now slide up and down the lip. Practice pushing off the balls of the feet, leaning back with the upper body, and looking with the head. Think about extending up off the lip, then bringing the shins up into your hands to speed the

spin. On your first Back Somersault, the first thing you should see is your landing.

4. Have your coach tell you where to start on the inrun. Select some signal the coach can shout such as "Tuck" if a crash is inevitable. If that occurs, go into an immediate tuck with the head between the knees and arms. This is a protective position and helps prevent any serious injury. Then work out a system of voice cues so your coach can talk to you through the maneuver. Select just a few words such as "Feet!" "Hips!" and "Look!" These will emphasize the timing and the key points.

5. At the starting point on the inrun, mentally review the voice cues and steps of the complete somersault. Concentrate on the exact body movements—not "I'll try it this time." "It" is too vague! Concentrate on the specific requirements of the jump. When you are ready, push off and drop your poles. Concentrate on the first thing you are going to do. Listen for the voice cue. Start your hands forward to begin the action. Rock forward onto the balls of the feet, extending the legs, thrusting the hips up and forward, and bend back looking for your landing. Bring the knees up to the hands and grasp them. When you see the landing, judge when to release your knees and extend your body to slow the spin for the landing.

BACK SOMERSAULT IN LAYOUT POSITION

6. Immediately review the maneuver after landing and stopping. Analyze your movements during the maneuver. Did you perform the key movements? Now fix up your landing area. Add some more soft snow for a cushion and climb to the top again. Review again at the top of the inrun before your next attempt.

ERROR CORRECTION

1. Avoid pushing your feet ahead to create the backward bend. This puts you on your heels, increasing the chances of hitting the back of your head on the take-off, and causes a quick somersault that is difficult to control. Emphasize thrusting the hips forward and pushing off the balls of the feet.

2. Underspinning or stalling in the air can be caused by not initiating the somersaulting action on the ramp, failing to extend the legs on initiation while pushing the hips up-forward, not looking with the head, and failing to tuck.

3. Twisting can be caused by pushing harder off one foot, turning the head and shoulders, or leaning to the side. Stress equally weighted skis on the initiation and working both sides of the body equally.

4. Keep your eyes open to time your landing. Remember the feet can hit the snow just a little behind the body because the direction of spin will push the skis right under the hips.

5. Avoid using poles for first attempts. They can aid balance if properly used, but it gives you one more thing to think about, and it is possible to land on them during a fall.

6. Skiers commonly drop their hands to their legs to form the tuck position. Bring your legs and knees upward to your hands.

BACK SOMERSAULT IN LAYOUT POSITION

The Back Somersault in the layout position is initiated in the same manner as the tuck somersault. Instead of pulling the legs up, the hips continue to press upward. The head and shoulders drive back toward the landing. The arms are pointed straight out to the side. The movement of the hips is more forceful to compensate for the slow spin in the layout position. It is extremely difficult to complete a Back Somersault in the layout position without bending at the

waist or overspinning. All of the spin comes from the initiation on the jump. There are very few ways to alter speed once the spin has been initiated. The speed of a layout somersault can be increased slightly by an extreme arching of the back because it brings the head and feet closer to the spin axis, or it can be slowed by remaining as straight as possible and extending the arms overhead to lengthen the body. On initiation, the timing of the spin must be very close to perfect. The aerialist must have excellent judgment in determining the amount of air time and the rate of spin to avoid bending at the knees or waist.

SIDE SOMERSAULT
(Loop)

The Side Somersault on skis was developed more recently than the Front or Back Somersault, and was popularized by Ed Lincoln. The Side Somersault is a unique maneuver because the aerialist can see his landing area or focus point during the entire somersault, enabling a jumper to make adjustments for the land-

SIDE SOMERSAULT IN TUCK POSITION

ing immediately after becoming airborne. In the Side Somersault, the hips and feet go out to the side so the body spins on the frontal axis of the body (see Appendix). When the Side Somersault is done in a tuck, the aerialist is in an excellent protective position in the event of a crash.

DESCRIPTION

At the top of the inrun, select a focus point to view during the entire maneuver. Following a pushoff and dropping of the poles to the snow, stand in a balanced position on both feet, with the body perpendicular to the pull of gravity when the skis begin to climb the takeoff. To initiate a Side Somersault to the left, spring off both feet, with a more forceful push off the right foot (outside foot) in a smooth fluid motion to move the hips out to the right side. The head and shoulders drop down to the left, creating a sideways

arch. The arms assist this action by circling counterclockwise, the right arm moving up and the left arm dropping down. The head and chest continue to face forward to avoid any twisting of the body. In the air, the legs are bent in close to the hips to increase the speed of the spin. The eyes continue to look at the focus point in the landing area as the body spins in a somersault. When the somersault is nearly completed, the body extends to slow the rotation and the feet are set down right under the hips.

LEARNING STEPS

1. As in all aerial maneuvers, any related gymnastic activity will improve your feeling for a maneuver and give you a good air sense. Cartwheels are especially functional in developing the Side Somersaults, particularly when used on a springboard, trampoline, and minitrampoline. The key points to strive for

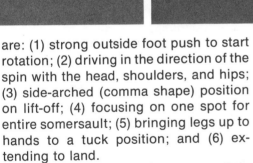

are: (1) strong outside foot push to start rotation; (2) driving in the direction of the spin with the head, shoulders, and hips; (3) side-arched (comma shape) position on lift-off; (4) focusing on one spot for entire somersault; (5) bringing legs up to hands to a tuck position; and (6) extending to land.

2. The contour of the lip does very little to assist the action of a Side Somersault. An abrupt lip can throw an aerialist off balance to the front or back. A long, smooth Back Somersault jump with little "kick" is most popular.

3. Observe other jumpers doing Side Somersaults. Slide up and down the lip, practicing the initiation of the Side Somersault, spotting on an object. Imagine the world turning upside down as you think through the Side Somersault.

4. On your first attempts, it may help to ski down the inrun with the left arm high and the right arm low. Then raise the

right and lower the left arm during the initiation. This wind-up with the arms will get your shoulders going in the right direction. Try to push off stronger with your right foot to get the spin started. If a mishap occurs, go into a tuck with your head between your knees and your arms drawn in close.

ERROR CORRECTION

1. The most common error is twisting off the frontal axis so the skier lands at an angle to the intended direction of travel. The twist is usually caused by turning the head, chest, or hips out of perpendicular alignment with the focus point. Emphasize a straight sideward lean, keeping the chest facing squarely downhill and concentrate on the focus point.

2. Aerialists who travel sideways through the air must work on developing a sideways arched position during the initiation. Most frequently, leaning to the side without counterbalancing by moving the hips out to the other side will cause a distorted flight. Sometimes a crooked flight is caused by pushing more vigorously off the inside foot, which creates the off-balanced lean to the side.

3. Underspinning is usually caused by lack of leg extension and failure to lean to the side with the upper body to start the initiation. Emphasize the circular action of the arms and a vigorous pushoff.

Inverted Aerials can be dangerous. Taking all the necessary precautions and learning the lead-up stunts are the best methods of reducing dangers. Most experts who are still jumping have done just that. They have found a way to practice without taking unnecessary risks.

Variations of the Front, Back, and Side Somersault are becoming more common. Crossing the tails of the skis, putting the hands in an unusual position, adding Spreads, Daffies, Double Spreads, and Back Scratchers have all been incorporated into the somersault routines. Mastery of the fundamentals, development of muscular control, and confidence open the door to these new adventures. Practice until you know where you are in the air and then begin experimentation. You are limited only by your understanding of the principles of somersaulting and your desire to improve. But, remember, make the learning conditions as safe as possible.

10
TWISTING AERIALS

In many ways, the principles of somersaulting relate directly to the principles of twisting, only in this case the rotation is around the vertical or longitudinal axis of the body (Illustration, p. 168). Once the basic principles of twisting are mastered, an endless variety of combination jumps can be attempted. Aerialists are now doing Full Twisting Tip Drops, Full Twisting Front and Reverse Somersaults, Helicopters in Spreads, and 720s. What will develop in the years to come will be limited only by the creativity of the mind and the physical capabilities of the body.

The principles of twisting are quite complex. A small book could be written on the subject if a detailed, technical analysis were the intended purpose. Furthermore, an extensive familiarity with physics and kinesiology would be necessary to comprehend and appreciate an in-depth analysis of this nature. The following analysis, although brief, will communicate a simple understanding of the key elements involved in executing a twisting motion as it relates to aerials.

THE PRINCIPLES OF TWISTING

There are three principal axes of the human body: the longitudinal or twist axis roughly parallel to the spine, the lateral or somersault axis, and the frontal or "side somersault" axis running front to back (see Glossary). If rotation were to take place about only one of these axes, the result would be a pure Twist (Helicopter), pure Somersault, or pure Side Somersault. The more complex aerials involve rotations about more than one axis, and as explained in the Appendix, usually some rotation exists about all three axes in such complex motions because of the difficulty of initiating only twisting on the longitudinal axis during a somersault. Therefore, the primary interest here is to understand twisting motions (i.e., rotation about the longitudinal axis), since these are far more commonly used in conjunction with forward and backward somersaulting.

A twisting motion can be initiated by several methods or even a combination of methods. To simplify our analysis of

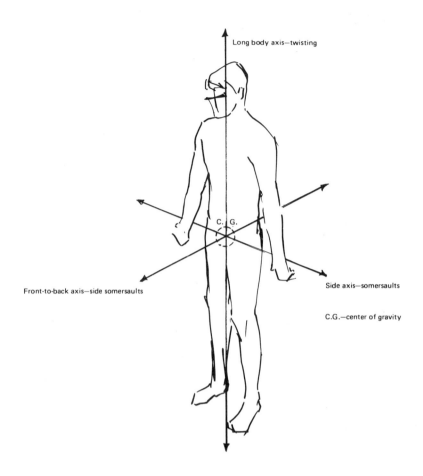

Long body axis—twisting

Front-to-back axis—side somersaults

Side axis—somersaults

C.G.—center of gravity

the differences between each method, we have divided twisting into two main categories: twists started with the feet in contact with the ski jump, and twists started with the feet in the air.

TWISTS STARTED ON THE SKI JUMP

The most common method aerialists use to initiate a twist is to begin the twisting action while the skis are still on the jump. In this case the head, shoulders, and arms are turned very hard in the direction of the twist. (See the photographs of the initiations for the Helicopter, Full Twisting Front and Full Twisting Back Somersault.) With the upper body already twisting rapidly in one direction while the lower body is externally stabilized by the jump, the angular momentum of the upper body is transferred to the hips, legs, and skis once they leave

the jump and are free to follow. The speed of the twist can be increased by wrapping the arms in close to the body or by taking advantage of additional methods of twisting that can be initiated in the air.

Twists begun on the jump are easy to visualize because a skier can feel his upper body turn, trying to pull the lower body in the same direction. The timing is critical because the upper body must be twisting as the skis leave the jump. If the upper body is stationary because of a late initiation, or because the twist was started too soon and the body stopped as it reached its natural limits of flexibility, then the aerialist will become "stuck" in the air. Twisting begun on the jump seems to be one of the best methods of twisting because a strong initiation helps to overcome the handicap created by

TWISTS STARTED ON THE JUMP

wearing skis and boots. (For the influence of skis and boots on twisting aerials, see the Appendix.)

Other methods of twisting are possible, primarily involving moving the arms and changing the body position in the air. These methods work extremely well for gymnasts and divers, but skiers are severely handicapped because of the additional weight and length of the skis and boots. The center of gravity is lowered dramatically by an increase of weight at one end of the body. The additional length of the skis perpendicular to the body increases the moment of inertia about the longitudinal axis and slows down the speed of the twist. Accordingly, skiers attempting any full 360-degree twisting maneuvers should concentrate on a strong initiation while the skis are still in contact with the jump if the maneuver calls for one or more complete rotations in the air.

TWISTING ACTIONS STARTED IN THE AIR

Aerialists use several different methods, sometimes in combination, to initiate some types of twisting action in the air. Primarily, they use the forces of action and reaction in Upright Aerials to produce a half or quarter twist before untwisting or realigning skis and body to prepare for the landing, as in a Twister or

Side Kick. A twisting action can also be initiated by tipping the body sideways off the somersaulting axis from a pike or arched position.

Action-Reaction Twisting: Action-reaction twisting is a prime example of Newton's Law of Motion—for every action there is an equal and opposite reaction. Once an aerialist is in the air, if the skis are turned in one direction the arms and upper body will twist in the opposite direction. When the body reaches its natural limit of torsional flexibility it begins to untwist, returning to its original position. The untwisting action may be conscious or automatic; since conscious muscle effort is required to hold the twisted position, simple relaxation will cause the unwinding to take place. A complete 360-degree twist around the longitudinal body axis does not take place as a result of such action initiated in the air. To complete a 360-degree twist by initiation in the air, a different set of actions is required as explained in the Appendix. The method described here is rarely satisfactory for anything more than a quarter to a half twist, which returns back to the starting position before landing.

Twisting By Tipping the Body Sideways Off the Somersaulting Axis: More difficult to visualize, the twisting action ini-

ACTION-REACTION TWISTING

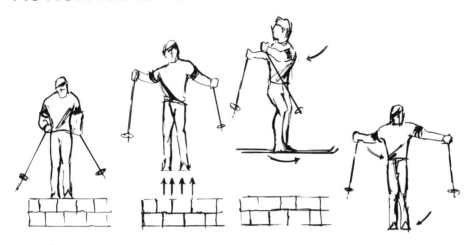

tiated by tipping the body off the spin axis is possible only if the aerialist is somersaulting. An asymmetrical object somersaulting in space will twist as well as somersault if it is tilted, tipped, or bent off the spin axis. As an example, throw a heavy-headed hammer somersaulting into the air with a slight diagonal tilt. It is virtually impossible to prevent it from twisting as it spins. Since humans can change the position of their body parts relative to one another, it is possible to tilt sideways during a somersault, thereby creating an asymmetrical position that will facilitate twisting. Gymnasts and divers can create this effect by circular motion of the arms as described in the Appendix. Since the arms have very little mass in comparison with the rest of the body and can generate limited angular momentum in comparison with the additional mass and length of the skis on the opposite end of the body, the effectiveness of the arm action for tilting the body off the spin axis is reduced for the Freestyler. Therefore, in order to make maximum use of the asymmetry principle for twisting, it seems necessary for aerialists to create this position by tilting the body out to the side at takeoff to take advantage of the additional twisting action that can be created.

Twisting out of a pike or arched position is an excellent example of twisting initiated by tipping the body sideways off the somersaulting axis. Sometimes aerialists will kink sideways at the hips to help complete that last quarter twist they need. Some specific examples of body actions are reviewed to illustrate why this works: If an aerialist jumps off a lip in a straight-up position without twisting or spinning, he cannot twist by turning his upper body in one direction because his legs will twist in the opposite direction (action-reaction: Newton). Similarly, if an aerialist jumps and pikes in the air after a straight-up initiation and then thrusts his upper body to one side, his legs and skis will move in the opposite direction to counterbalance. Still, no twist can occur because spin is missing. But if an aerialist is spinning in a piked or arched position and then twists his upper body out to the side, rapid twisting will occur because an asymmetrical position has been created during somersaulting. There is growing evidence to support the theory that tilting off the spin axis in somersaults is responsible for the fastest possible twisting action for divers and gymnasts (Batterman). Whether or not this holds true for an aerialist remains to be seen. The increased weight of the skis and boots coupled with the drag created by the length of the skis may substantially reduce this action of tilting off the spin axis.

TWIST INITIATIONS IN SOMERSAULTS

When first learning twisting in somersaults, emphasize the initiation of twisting on the jump by a movement of the arms, shoulders, and head in the direction of the twist. Then, as skill and confidence increase, the concept of tilting off the somersault axis may be attempted. Many times skiers learn this concept inadvertently when they are "saving" a short twist or somersault by bending rapidly sideways at the waist in the direction of the twist to bring their skis around so they can land completing the twist. This saving action is also characterized by a movement of the arms across the midline of the body opposite to the direction of the intended twist (action-reaction) to complete the final quarter turn.

CONTROLLING THE SPEED OF TWISTS

During the twist, the body turns on its longitudinal axis. The closer the arms, legs, and body are held to straight-bodied position, the faster the twist. Conversely, if the arms and legs are spread and bending at the waist occurs, the speed of the twist will be substantially reduced. Twisting is done in two basic positions, the layout position and the free position. In executing a single stunt, both positions may be used at different times during the sequence of movements.

The Layout Position: In the layout position, the body is extended to a completely straight position in order to align as closely as possible with the longitudinal axis. The back is straight, the legs are straight, and the arms are held close to the body. A twist in the layout position may start with the arms extended out to the sides at right angles to the length of the body. Then the arms are brought in close to increase the speed of the twist. To slow the twist and prepare for landing, the arms, and possibly the legs, are extended to the side.

The Free Position: The free position is a catch-all term used to describe the changing body positions that may occur during twisting somersaults to control the speed of the twist and/or the spin. This changing position is commonly seen in the Full Twisting Front Somersault. The Twisting Front Somersault is initiated on the jump by a turning of the body in the direction of the twist, and with an extending of the legs going immediately into a pike position. Then the body straightens to slow the speed of the somersault and increase the speed of the twisting motion. At the proper moment, the twisting is slowed by bending slightly into an open-pike position. This increases the speed of the somersault to complete the spinning action and prepare for landing. Mastery of the free position depends upon learning to judge the forces of twisting in the somersault, so that an aerialist knows when to slow one action to increase the speed of the other movement.

Ski Length: The length of the ski also affects the speed of a twist. The shorter the ski, the smaller effect it has on the moment of inertia about the longitudinal axis of the body. Shorter skis will twist faster with the same amount of initiating force. However, the major obstacle in using shorter skis is the difficulty encountered when trying to land balanced. Longer skis provide more stability during impact. Aerialists must compromise between the desire to twist quickly and the need to land with greater stability when selecting ski length for aerials.

FORMATION OF THE TAKEOFF

In Aerial Acrobatics, twisting may occur in both the Upright Aerials and the Inverted Aerials. Formation of the contour of the takeoff is determined by whether the stunt is an Upright or an Inverted Aerial. Upright Twisting Aerials require gentle floater lips that promote balance in an Upright position. Twisting somersaults require a takeoff that facilitates the initiation of the somersault. Detailed

TWISTER

descriptions of these takeoffs are found in Chapter 8, "Upright Aerials."

PRELIMINARY EXERCISES FOR TWISTING AERIALS

There are a variety of activities and equipment that can be used to teach a person how to twist. Some are better suited to the development of twisting in Upright Aerials, others lend themselves to learning the twist in Inverted Aerials. All of these activities should be attempted and mastered before trying them with skis to avoid the bone-rattling crashes that occur with failures.

The trampoline and overhead twisting belt can be used safely and effectively for both Upright and Inverted Aerials with twists. The trampoline allows for large amounts of practice in a short period of time in the safest conditions. When a trampoline with a spotting belt is unavailable, a diving board or mini-trampoline is our next preference. Preliminary to all workouts, practice the twisting–stretching exercises in Chapter 1, "Accelerate Learning Safely."

TWISTER

The Twister could have been properly included in the chapter on Upright Aerials, since it is similar to the Side Kick and requires the same method of initiation—straight up! However, this stunt was placed with Twisting Aerials to emphasize the important difference between initiations of twists. The Twister is a good example of action-reaction twisting. The action of the stunt is initiated in the air after takeoff: a quarter to half twist occurs while the upper body counteracts the movement of the lower body unwinding before landing. A Helicopter, which requires a 360 Twist, is initiated on the jump so the feet are stabilized during the initial rotary action of the upper body. Note the difference—a Twister is initiated in the air. Start a Twister too soon and it will end up being a half-twisting crash.

DESCRIPTION

Using the same takeoff as for all Upright

Aerials, a straight-up initiation is made. Once in the air, the legs and feet are turned so the skis point at right angles to the direction of travel. At the same time, the arms swing across and/or the head and upper body turn in the opposite direction to maintain balance in the air. This position is held for a moment, then the legs and arms untwist to the original position, facing in the direction of travel. In an emergency, the speed of this action can be increased by using muscle power to turn the legs back to the straight-ahead position. The impact is absorbed by bending at the ankles, knees, and hips.

LEARNING STEPS

1. Practice jumping straight into the air off a small rise or mogul. Once in the air, turn the legs under the body so the feet point to one side. Balance by simultaneously turning the upper body in the opposite direction, or swinging the arms across or pulling back the opposite shoulder. Return everything to its original position before landing.

2. Before your first jump, review by standing on one leg and turning the other in the desired direction while keeping the boots under the hips. Try it first off little jumps, working up to larger jumps as confidence increases.

ERROR CORRECTION

1. The most common error is initiating the twisting action on the jump, resulting in a crooked takeoff and a slow twist that is difficult to correct before landing. It is important to remember that the Twister is an Upright Aerial and is initiated after takeoff.

2. A partial twist in the air can also result from not counterbalancing the leg and ski movement with an arm or upper body movement in the opposite direction. Style may vary in the way the aerialist counterbalances for the turning of the legs, but counterbalancing must occur to remain balanced in the air.

3. Those experiencing difficulty in maintaining a vertical position in the air can raise one or both arms to lengthen the longitudinal axis of the body to prevent a slow somersaulting off the vertical axis. Frequently this raised arm position is incorporated as a planned movement in the maneuver to assure balance in the air. Because the arms now are aligned with the body longitudinal axis, the upper body must turn more vigorously to counterbalance the actions of the legs.

HELICOPTER
(Chopper 360)

The Helicopter is the first aerial in which the twist is initiated on the jump and a complete spin about the longitudinal axis of the body occurs in the air. The Helicopter is a versatile maneuver that is used in all the Freestyle events. The basic mechanics involved in the timing of the initiation remain the same regardless of where Helicopters are done. In

HELICOPTER

fact, the twisting action is quite useful when experimenting with new Ballet maneuvers on either one or both feet.

DESCRIPTION

Usually a focus point is selected in the landing area to serve as a signal to slow the speed of the twist and adjust for the landing. Ski down the inrun balanced on both feet. Prepare for the spring by flexing the ankles and knees. The twisting action is begun by turning the head, shoulders, and arms in the direction of the twist while the feet push against the jump and the legs extend for height. The twisting extension of the body should be such that the body remains straight in alignment, with the ski boots under the hips, shoulders, and head. Once in the air, the arms are wrapped in close to the body to increase the speed of the twist. The head continues to turn, looking over the shoulder in the direction of the twist for the focus point in the landing area. When the focus point is spotted, the arms extend to slow the speed of the twist and prepare for landing.

LEARNING STEPS

1. The twisting extension that initiates the Helicopter can be practiced on a trampoline, or by just jumping into the air off the ground. Once on the snow, learn the last half of the Helicopter first. Practice jumping from a stationary position and turning 180 degrees. Try a preliminary windup with the arms and upper body to put more momentum into the twisting action. Emphasize looking over your shoulder for the previously selected focus point.

2. The first attempt while skiing should be done across a hill rather than down it. A small mogul with a smooth flat takeoff should be used to provide the necessary air time. The twist should be initiated uphill, so the body turns uphill first. This provides a greater margin for successful landings even if the Helicopter is under-

twisted. Start at a slow speed and turn uphill, sinking in the ankles and knees so the skis are aimed straight up the hill before initiating the twist. Then initiate the twist as you jump by twisting the head and torso in the direction you want to rotate. The initiation should be timed so the body is straight and the upper body is turning rapidly as the skis leave the ground. As your skill increases, decrease the degree to which you turn uphill before initiation. Eventually you should be able to ski straight across the hill, hit a small mogul and complete a 360 Spin in the air without a preliminary turn up the hill.

3. Once a Helicopter can be done while skiing across the hill, increase the steepness of the line so you aim more down the hill.

4. When first trying a twist off a jump, build a smooth takeoff and a landing area with very little drop, if any, to decrease the impact caused by falling from a height if a mistake occurs. As skill increases, gradually cut away the landing area until you are doing Helicopters off a regular jump.

ERROR CORRECTION

1. A common error is failing to maintain a straight position with the feet, hips, back, and head all in vertical alignment. Bending at the waist or tilting the body out of alignment results in a slower twist and a weak initiation. Several things can be done to correct this problem. The inside pole should be planted on the lip close to the skis to remind you to keep your back straight, and to signal the start of the twisting extension of the initiation. Emphasize looking over the shoulder rather than around it to help keep the chest up and the back straight. One arm can be thrust high into the air to assist the extension and to lengthen the body to help prevent tipping.

2. Underspinning is usually caused by poor timing during the initiation. The twisting action must be started on the lip

and must be present during lift-off. If the twisting action is late or after the lift-off, there is nothing to push against to get the twist started. The opposite also holds true: if the twisting action was initiated too early and is completed or almost stopped before takeoff, a slow quarter twist will occur in the air. This is a very difficult position to land in safely. A pole plant can be used to time the twisting extension so the body is turning just at takeoff. Underspinning can also be caused if the arms and legs are spread. They should be wrapped in close to the body to increase the speed of the twist. Spreading the extremities helps to provide balance in the air or slow a spin, but it does little to help complete it.

3. Tilting off balance in the air can usually be traced back to the initiation. The upward twisting extension must be straight up, away from the pull of gravity. The center of gravity must stay directly over the feet. A lean in any direction or a bend at the waist can cause an off-balance position. Dipping the shoulders or head during the initiation will also cause an unbalanced flight. The focus point can be spotted on the initiation to help align the body in the air, followed by a quick turning of the head to look for it the second time when in the air. Reaching forward in a circular motion toward the focus point with the outside arm also may help to stabilize the body position in the air as the jump is initiated.

After takeoff, the arm can be brought in to increase the speed of the spin.

4. Overspinning is usually caused by a twisting action too strong for the amount of air time. The twist can be slowed by spreading the arms, and even the legs if necessary. If overspinning is still a problem, the focus point can be spotted when leaving the jump while the body is twisting underneath. Then the head can be turned quickly to catch up to the body and find the focus point again. The arms should be unwrapped and the legs spread to slow the spin.

AXIAL

The Axial is borrowed directly from ice skating and is used primarily in Ballet. It is an aerial maneuver because a 360 Spin is done completely in the air. The Axial starts on one foot and ends on the other after completing one or more revolutions. It is simply a Helicopter started on the inside ski and finished on the outside ski.

DESCRIPTION

To prepare for the initiation, the upper body is wound up opposite to the intended direction of spin. The upper body starts unwinding rapidly in the direction of the spin initiating a One-Ski 360 Spin on the inside/uphill ski. The inside pole may be planted to time the lift-off, which

AXIAL

occurs immediately by extending the leg and hopping off the weighted ski. The head and upper body continue to turn in the direction of the spin, looking for the landing or focus point. The skis are brought together in the air to increase the speed of the twist. Once the spin is completed, land only on the outside/downhill foot.

LEARNING STEPS

1. Review the Helicopter. Practice landing on the outside/downhill ski to get the feeling of landing on one foot and to learn the end of the turn first.

2. Now initiate a Helicopter by pushing harder off the inside/uphill ski. Land on both feet. Keep repeating this exercise, increasing the weight on the inside/uphill ski until the maneuver can be initiated on one foot.

3. Then put these two exercises together: the result will be an Axial. If problems develop, try the learning sequence that follows.

4. While moving slowly across the hill, start a 360 Spin on the inside/uphill ski. When you have spun 180 degrees, do a Downhill Stepover while traveling backwards. Do the Stepover so as to turn the remaining 180 degrees, so you are facing the original direction of travel.

5. Now try the same thing with a hop off the weighted ski. Get the feeling of pushing off hard in the direction of the spin, looking with your head and upper body.

6. Do it again, but this time turn up the hill only 90 degrees; then, with a hard push, spin and do the Downhill Stepover. The timing is very important. As soon as the spin is started, the foot must push off with sufficient lift to complete the spin in the air.

7. Once the timing is mastered, you can stop thinking of the Axial as a Downhill Stepover. Now try to push off the uphill foot and bring the skis together in the air. Land on both feet. First try to spin half way before going for a full 360 Axial.

8. As skill improves, emphasize landing with more weight on the downhill ski. Then try to land on the downhill foot. When the one-foot landing is mastered, you may find it hard to stop the raised foot from spinning because of the momentum of the ski and boot. To get around this problem, try letting the raised uphill ski continue to swing into another maneuver such as a Shea-Guy, 360 Royal, Crossbehind, etc. When attempting Axials with more than a 360-degree spin, try to land on both feet in the beginning. Personal flair can be added after the maneuver is mastered.

ERROR CORRECTION

1. Leaning to the inside is a common problem. The head and shoulders should be kept level while standing directly over the skis, otherwise the body begins to tilt in the air resulting in an off-balance posi-

FULL TWISTING
FRONT SOMERSAULT

tion. A vertical pole plant can remind you to keep your back straight.

2. If you have difficulty completing the 360 in the air, work backwards, learning the end of the maneuver first by turning farther uphill before initiating the hop.

FULL TWISTING FRONT SOMERSAULT
(Front Moebius)

A Full Twisting Somersault is one of the most difficult of all the aerial maneuvers. The aerialist must maintain an awareness of body positioning on at least two planes during the entire maneuver. It is easy to become confused and "lost" in this maneuver. Soft snow, a steep landing area, luck, and a protective tuck position are many times the only things that prevent serious injury. The Full Twisting Somersault should be completely mastered on trampolines and diving boards before even a thought is given to attempting it on skis.

The Full Twisting Front Somersault is a difficult stunt to perform consistently. It is considered a blind maneuver, since the aerialist usually sees the landing just a split second before impact, allowing little time to make any last moment adjustments. However, the twisting action allows the aerialist to view the landing area for a somewhat longer period of time than in a regular Front Somersault. The eyes can focus downwards as the body twists and somersaults. Then, just before impact, the head is raised and twisted in the direction of the intended landing. An aerialist who uses a focus point (dye or tree boughs) immediately below his intended trajectory can more easily determine his relative body position during the maneuver.

DESCRIPTION
On the inrun, the body is slightly flexed in a balanced position. The hands are carried at approximately chest height, slightly forward and outside the line of the body. When the skis climb the take-off, the body leans forward and the legs are extended to push the hips up as the head, arms, and shoulders begin rotating in the direction of the twist. A twist in a counterclockwise direction can be assisted by pushing harder on the right foot. The head, arms, and shoulders rotate downward immediately as the legs push off the jump.

Once in the air, the lower body and skis begin to follow the initial twisting action of the upper body as the arms are wrapped in close to the body to increase the speed of the twist. The legs are sub-

sequently pushed up behind the body to a layout position. The eyes focus on a spot in the landing area directly below the body. Then, when the twist is almost complete, the eyes, head, and upper body are shifted away from the initial focus point and face forward down the outrun to complete the twist and raise the head. The arms spread and the body bends at the waist to slow the twisting action and complete the somersault. The final actions or body positions may be altered by varying degrees to compensate for differences in the speed of twist or somersault. The focus point and kinesthetic feel provide the information necessary to determine final adjustments before impact.

LEARNING STEPS

1. Before a Full Twisting Front Somersault is attempted on snow, you should be able to perform consistently the following maneuvers: (1) Front Somersaults in the pike and layout positions with skis on; (2) a Helicopter and a Full Twisting Front Somersault on the trampoline, diving board, and mini-trampoline. You must develop a feeling of where you are in the air, acquired through continual practice. Use a focus point to improve body orientation in the air.

2. At the ski area, build a jump with a steep landing and pad it with plenty of soft snow. Draw a line down the center of the landing area in the direction of travel to be used as a focus point during the maneuver. A line is necessary because the body travels over a long distance and it is hard to focus on one point.

3. Do several Front Layouts to determine where to start on the inrun. Then review the actions of a Full Twisting Front Somersault by taking off your skis and doing several off a mini-trampoline.

4. Then, with your skis on, slide slowly up the takeoff, practicing the initiation. Imagine yourself taking off and completing the maneuver. Work out some voice cues with your spotter to remind you of key movements or to warn you of any impending danger so you can go into a protective spread-knee tuck.

5. At the top of the inrun, mentally review the key factors, emphasizing the initiation of the twist and somersault on the jump. Think of leaning forward and extending off the balls of the feet as the hands, head, and upper body begin the twisting action. It may help to wind up with the arms in a counter motion as you are sliding down the inrun. Then the arms and upper body can be thrown more vigorously into the twist to increase momentum.

6. Immediately after the first attempt review your actions. Think about what you felt, how your body moved and responded in the air. Talk with your spotter. Try to visualize your first experience and look for ways to improve your second attempt. Remember, a Full Twisting Front Somersault is a difficult stunt to master because it has a blind landing.

ERROR CORRECTION

1. Frequent difficulty is encountered because skiers lack skill in the basic maneuvers that are the necessary prerequisites for this maneuver. If the skier fails to extend off the lip (something he should have learned in a Front Somersault), the initiation for the twist as well as the somersault will be weak, if not completely absent. When problems occur, see if the difficulty can be worked out in a maneuver that involves less risk.

2. The initiation of the twist and the somersault occur in a simultaneously coordinated action when the skis are still on the jump. If they are not initiated at the same time, the skier will somersault without the twist or twist without completing the somersault.

3. A half-twisting somersault is usually a result of a weak initiation or a failure to shift the eyes from the first focus point in the landing area to a position looking down the outrun. Remember, there are *two* focus points in this maneuver. The first should be located directly below the aerialist (the line on the snow) as he twists and somersaults during the majority of the maneuver. The second should be the end of the outrun or the horizon line so it pulls his head around to help complete the last part of the twist.

4. A loss of orientation occurs if the eyes are taken off the focus point. The problem is caused by throwing the twist too early or keeping the chin in as the body reaches a vertical upside-down position. The first focus point should be viewed during the majority of the maneuver, then the eyes are quickly shifted from it to a forward position to complete the twist and land.

5. Lifting the head and arms to gain height on the initiation is another common error. Remember, the lift comes from the extension of the legs pushing the hips into the air and the kick provided by the jump. The arms and upper body should begin rotating across and down so the legs can be immediately snapped over the head to a layout position to speed the twisting action.

6. Some aerialists have such a strong initiation they do not have to wrap their arms close to their body to increase the speed of the twist (see photograph). Others need to keep the arms in tight to the body to assure a complete twist. The arms can be wrapped next to the body in many different ways: the exact placement of the arms has very little effect on Twisting Somersaults because the added weight of the skis and boots helps to nullify any movement and/or change of position of the arms while in the air.

FULL TWISTING BACK SOMERSAULT
(Back Moebius)

A Full Twisting Back Somersault allows the aerialist to spot the landing area early In the somersault so it is kept in view during the majority of the maneuver. As a result, a natural focus point is provided and the aerialist is allowed an extra period of time in which to make the necessary adjustments to assure a balanced landing. Accordingly, this stunt is generally more popular than the Full Twisting Front Somersault, although the body is more vulnerable to injury if a mistake is made when the body is in the arched or straight position. The Full Twisting Back Somersault is performed off the same shaped lip as for regular Back Somersaults to provide the proper lift to assist the initiation of the somersault.

DESCRIPTION

A Full Twisting Back Somersault begins in the same starting position as a layout Back Somersault. The hands are carried at waist height and out to the side during the inrun. As the skis begin to climb the takeoff, the hands and hips start forward ahead of the upper body as the legs extend by pushing off the balls of the feet. Simultaneously, the head, arms, and shoulders begin rotating in the direction of the twist as the back is arched. To twist counterclockwise, the aerialist pushes harder off the right foot as the right arm reaches up for height and circles in the direction of the twist while the left arm reaches back. The eyes look back over the left shoulder toward the snow. All these actions are initiated while the skis are still in contact with the jump. Immediately upon becoming airborne, the lower body and skis begin to follow the initial twisting motion of the upper body. The arms are wrapped in close to increase the speed of the twist. The landing area is spotted immediately as the body twists and somersaults above it. Then, when the twist is almost completed, the arms (and possibly the legs) are spread to slow the twisting action and prepare for the landing. The head is raised and the eyes look down the outrun. The waist is bent slightly to bring the legs down to adjust for the landing.

LEARNING STEPS

1. Before this stunt is attempted on snow, master the basic moves on the trampoline and/or diving board. Then you should be able to perform consistently Helicopters and Back Layouts on skis until the movements are almost automatic with kinesthetic feeling for all these maneuvers. This will help prevent becoming "lost" in the air.

2. Next, build a Back Somersault jump that has a steep landing area and cover it with a deep blanket of soft snow. Practice Back Layouts to get a feel of the lip, and determine where to start on the inrun.

3. Then, with your skis on, slide slowly up the takeoff and practice the back initiation action on the lip of the jump. Concentrate on timing the actions so they are started on the jump and finish at the edge of the lip. Imagine what it will look like as you take off from the lip. Select a spot in the landing area to focus on during the maneuver to orient yourself in the air. Review voice cues with your spotter for timing and protection.

4. At the top of the inrun, mentally review the key factors, emphasizing the initiation on the jump. Think of rocking forward with the hips and extending off the balls of the feet as the upper body begins to rotate up and back while turning in the direction of the twist. Think of looking back and down for the focus point. Try to relax before you start down the inrun.

5. Immediately after the first attempt, mentally review your actions. Think through the total maneuver and how it

FULL TWISTING BACK SOMERSAULT

felt. Discuss what happened with your spotter and look for ways to improve your next attempt. Limit yourself to several attempts a day, particularly if you are experiencing difficulty.

ERROR CORRECTION

1. Frequently errors occur because skiers lack the basic skills in the lead-up stunts. Many times it is more beneficial to review the problem in another maneuver that provides practice of the necessary components with fewer dangers involved.

2. A late or early initiation results in the same corresponding errors that occur in Helicopters or Back Somersaults. The ini-tiation of the somersault and twist occur at the same time on the jump. The somersault usually is the easiest to achieve because of the assist from the takeoff. The initial twisting movement should be emphasized.

3. Disorientation can occur if the eyes are not looking at the landing area. This can also be caused by a weak twist that is not completed before three-fourths of the somersault is completed.

4. Bending the knees and leaning back on the heels during initiation can result in the head hitting the jump or a quick, uncontrolled somersault. Extend off the balls of the feet and arch backwards with the upper body to initiate the somersault.

5. Half-twisting somersaults are usually

a result of initiating late so the aerialist becomes "stuck" in the air. Another cause is failing to rotate the upper body powerfully enough in the direction of the twist while still on the jump. These actions should be reviewed on a trampoline. Remember, the speed of the somersault and twist can be varied by planned body movements that alter the body position in relationship to the central spinning axis. Shorter skis can also affect the speed of spin.

Aerials are fun. Lots of hard work and study are required to become a master in the air. Gone are the days of the devil-may-care competitor who goes for broke to win. The contests have become highly organized with fewer serious accidents.

Adding a few of these stunts to your repertoire of skills in skiing brings you that much closer to the feeling of freedom that wells up in us as we "get air." Join the ranks of the professionals. Get air safely.

11
COMPETITIVE GUIDELINES

Freestyle skiing was revolutionized by the organization and development of Freestyle competition and its exposure to the public. *Skiing* magazine sponsored national competitions and published this new form of hot dog skiing with eye-catching photographs and interesting articles. Filmmaker Dick Barrymore spread the word of this exciting type of competition to thousands of people through his movies. Sponsors provided cash awards and expensive prizes to the winners. "Hot" skiers found an outlet for their competitive spirits.

Freestyle skiing soon developed its own heros. Unknown competitors were attracted to the competitions to see if they could beat those heros whom they both respected and envied. Changes occurred very rapidly. The locally organized Freestyle competitions quickly became too large for a sponsor to operate with adequate safety standards. A standard set of organizational guidelines was needed to guide those who wished to sponsor a contest. Different organizational formats were tried and evaluated, and from these a basic outline developed consisting of one or more of the three

basic parts: Mogul skiing, Aerial Acrobatics, and Stunt and Ballet.

For each event, guidelines were established to standardize course preparation. All events were analyzed to determine what constituted the main criteria for evaluating a competitor's performance. A universal scoring system was developed to improve judging and help eliminate spectator confusion. As a result, contests became more uniformly organized and competition ran smoothly. Below is a brief analysis of each event with respect to hill preparation, basic procedures, and judging.

MOGUL EVENT

The Mogul event tests a competitor's free skiing ability—his courage, flexibility, balance, and ability to turn quickly. The course is laid out on a steep, heavily moguled slope where the moguls are usually sharper, shorter, and deeper than those typically found on gentler slopes. The carving and cutting action of shorter skis develops these knife-edged stairstep obstacles, making it much more difficult for a competitor to "find a line" through the bumps. Usually music is selected by

MOGUL EVENT COURSE CRITERIA

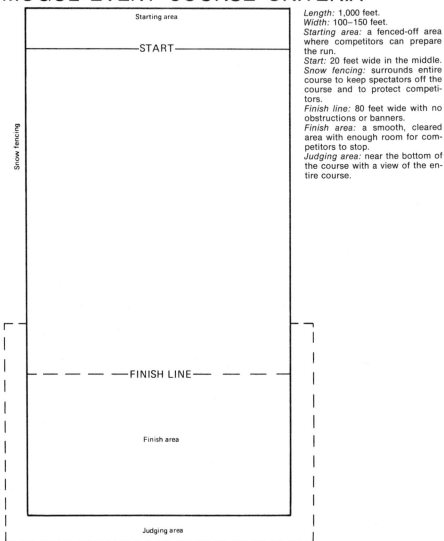

Starting area

START

Snow fencing

FINISH LINE

Finish area

Judging area

Length: 1,000 feet.
Width: 100–150 feet.
Starting area: a fenced-off area where competitors can prepare the run.
Start: 20 feet wide in the middle.
Snow fencing: surrounds entire course to keep spectators off the course and to protect competitors.
Finish line: 80 feet wide with no obstructions or banners.
Finish area: a smooth, cleared area with enough room for competitors to stop.
Judging area: near the bottom of the course with a view of the entire course.

the contestant to inspire his performance during the flight down the mountain.

Competitors are judged and given scores according to specific criteria. The Mogul event is evaluated according to the type of turns, the overall performance, speed, control, and continuity throughout the whole run. A competitor can boost his score by including difficult aerials in his run. However, air time must be executed smoothly and should not result in a loss of control. Falls or loss of control count heavily against a competi-

tor. A controlled stop must be made in the finish area to indicate to the judges the end of the run. A competitor is disqualified for loss of a ski or not finishing the course.

STUNT AND BALLET EVENT

The Stunt and Ballet event is similar to ice skating or creative dancing. It is a demonstration of intricate maneuvers and stunts combined artistically into smooth-flowing routines. Music almost always accompanies the performance, adding continuity and grace if the

BALLET EVENT COURSE CRITERIA

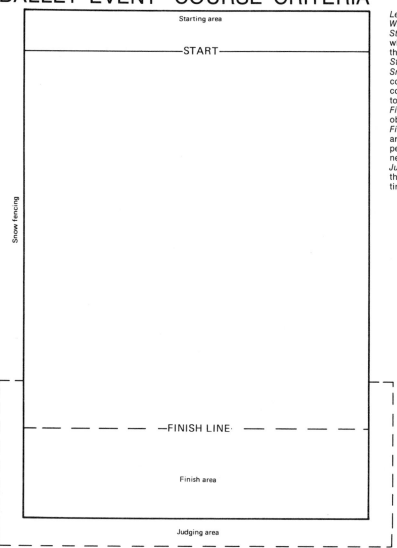

Starting area

——START——

Snow fencing

——FINISH LINE——

Finish area

Judging area

Length: 800 feet.
Width: 200 feet.
Starting area: a fenced-off area where competitors can prepare the run.
Start: 20 feet wide in the middle.
Snow fencing: surrounds entire course to keep spectators off the course and to protect competitors.
Finish line: 80 feet wide with no obstructions or banners.
Finish area: a smooth, cleared area with enough room for competitors to finish their routines, if necessary.
Judging area: near the bottom of the course with a view of the entire course.

maneuvers are done in time with the music.

Ballet routines may be spontaneous, but most competitors spend many hours practicing their own special routines using specially selected music. The amount of time spent practicing a single routine is reflected by the precision with which the stunts follow the music. Many competitors practice while listening to music on miniature cassette tape players through headphones.

Of the three events, Ballet allows greatest leeway for competitors to inno-

vate and invent new maneuvers and combinations of maneuvers. Many simple or basic tricks or stunts, when done in sequence, may make a beautiful Ballet routine. Even the novice competitor is given a chance to create a "dance" on snow and may generate a great amount of self-satisfaction. Although many of the same tricks may be used by different competitors, the different combination of the maneuvers make each routine unique.

Shorter skis with a soft flex and turned-up tails are generally used because of better maneuverability and lighter weight. Many tricks are not possible on longer skis. If the skis have a center groove, it is usually filled in with wax or P-tex. The grooves are not necessary for ballet skiing because the slow speeds at which the maneuvers are performed does not require the stability afforded by grooves at normal skiing speeds.

The use of ski poles in the ballet event is optional. Many competitors feel that the use of poles, while helping balance, restrict hand and arm movements that can be used to give maneuvers a finished look.

The Ballet competitor is judged on the difficulty and precision of the stunts executed. The overall performance is then considered by evaluating how well the whole routine was presented. Emphasis is placed on smoothness and continuity of performance. If music is used, its effect on the overall performance is also evaluated. A carefully choreographed routine set to music can raise the score. Falls or a loss of balance detract from a competitor's score. However, a competitor can only be disqualified for the loss of a ski.

Competitors do not have to cross the finish line to complete their routine. They are judged until they make a complete stop indicating the end of their routine. The stop can occur before the finish line or in the finish area. This feature is especially important when routines are done to music. A competitor tries to keep in time to the music, but varying weather and course conditions make it impossible to gauge accurately the length (in distance) of the routine. So the routine may end before or after the finish line depending on existing conditions.

AERIAL ACROBATIC EVENT

The Aerial Acrobatic event is a combination of ability and courage in aerial gymnastics. The coordination and control required to perform aerials makes this the most daring and spectacular of Freestyle events.

Extra care must be taken in the preparation of the Aerial Acrobatic courses. The event must be set up on special terrain, or Sno-cats must make the terrain suitable. Up to three jumps are built in series to form the aerial arena, each jump having a steep landing area. The inrun should be much more gradual (see jump construction). Therefore, the terrain on which an Aerial Acrobatic event is held must contain varying pitches with the jumps built in the correct locations. In a multi-jump contest, the jumps must be set far enough apart so competitors can gain their balance and have time to plan their next aerial maneuver.

Each jump is built with a variety of lips to accommodate the various types of aerial maneuvers. Upright jumps usually require a flatter takeoff than Inverted Aerials, which require a more abrupt spoon-shaped lip to help the competitor initiate his spin. The backsides of the jumps are often used by contest sponsors to display advertising banners.

The preparation of the Aerial Acrobatic course is more tedious than for any other event. Because of the greater possibility of injuries, it is imperative to see that all possible safety measures are taken to protect competitors. After the courses are set, they must be tested and all the competitors must be given an opportunity to make practice jumps to feel out the peculiarities of each jump. Snow and weather conditions vary from day to day, and competitors have to adjust to the conditions of the moment. A contest that does not follow all of the proper procedures to assure the competitors' safety may end in an unfortunate mishap.

In Aerial Acrobatics, competitors are judged strictly on the execution of their maneuvers. The judges consider only form in the air, distance, the height at which the maneuver is done, and the landing. A solid landing indicates the end of the maneuver. The difficulty of each maneuver is predetermined and given an appropriate numerical value. That value is multiplied by the judges' scores to determine the winner.

In a multi-jump contest, scores are awarded for each jump individually and the overall score is obtained by averaging the scores of all the jumps. This means well-rounded competitors usually obtain a higher overall score than the individual who has just one spectacular jump.

Falls count heavily against a competitor's score and can also be painful. To alleviate the problems of competitors "going for broke," emphasis is placed on precision and timing rather than how spectacular or appealing the maneuver is. Rigorous qualifications must also be passed prior to competition. Competitors must execute all the jumps that they intend to attempt in competition with enough confidence and ability to pass the competition qualification test. If a competitor attempts an unqualified maneuver, he will be immediately disqualified from competition, regardless of the outcome of the jump. Loss of a ski also results in disqualification.

In a multi-jump contest, competitors must ski from jump to jump, but are not judged during this portion of the run. Competitors may even stop during their run in order to set up for the next jump, and some contests require competitors to stop before each jump. Control gates are used to check the speed of the competitors. These precautions are needed to prevent competitors from getting too much height and/or distance for the attempted maneuver.

The Aerial Acrobatic event was the center of much controversy when the sport was first developing. Some unfortunate accidents received a great deal of publicity, which hurt the development of the Aerial Acrobatic event. Through work by the Freestyle organizations and sponsors and a sincere effort by competitors to police themselves against such accidents, the Aerial Acrobatic event is gaining credibility as the most exciting of athletic competitions.

In the preceding chapters we have presented a basic foundation and background for the newly created sport of Freestyle skiing. We realize our treatment of this subject encompasses only a small portion of the information available. Yet, as with every sport, there must be a place to begin. We have prepared this step-by-step description of the basic skills of Freestyle skiing so other skiers can experience the joys that result from venturing into a new realm and meeting with success.

We hope that you have sensed the importance of understanding body mechanics. Much of the technical information presented is based upon questions we have been asked by skiers of all ages and abilities. While the imitation method of learning provides satisfactory progress for many students, it is our firm belief that fast and efficient learning evolves only when there is a thorough understanding of the underlying mechanics of the maneuvers. It is the responsibility of serious skiers to become knowledgeable in this area so that Freestyle skiing may be a successful adventure in balance, efficiency, and creativity.

APPENDIX

In this Appendix by Dr. Juris Vagners some background material is presented for a more thorough understanding of the physics of rotational motion, neuromuscular control of movements, the balance mechanisms, and equilibrium concepts.

THE PHYSICS OF ROTATIONAL MOTION

To completely understand the why and wherefore of the different aerials, and why some particular movement is absolutely necessary for the successful completion of a particular stunt, the Freestyler must continually strive to broaden his knowledge of the underlying fundamentals. This Appendix by no means allows one to understand all of the intricacies and apparent "miracles" of rotational motion. However, the necessary definitions by key terms will be established, and some qualitative ideas presented about the physical laws governing motion and how these laws may be applied to a better understanding of Freestyle aerial movements. For more intensive study, interested readers should consult some of the numerous books available on mechanics (see Bibliogra-

phy for Appendix), with the caution that almost all publications on the fundamentals of mechanics require a facility and understanding of mathematics to varying degrees. An ability to reason and visualize abstractly is also required. In his comprehensive lectures on physics, the noted Nobel prize physicist Richard P. Feynman observed that "It will turn out, as we go to more and more advanced physics, that many simple things can be deduced mathematically more rapidly than they can be really understood in a fundamental or simple sense." Since no mathematical background is assumed on the part of the reader, some things will have to be taken for granted as absolute truth, with the faith that, indeed, the results can be deduced mathematically by those so trained, as well as verified experimentally.

The first concept to explore is the validity of considering the rotational motion of a body in space independently of its general translation in space. What is meant by this is most simply explained by visualizing the motion of a rectangular block of clear plastic thrown through the air. Draw the axis of symmetry of the block as shown in the sketch and mark

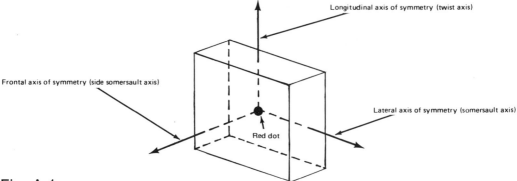

Fig. A-1

the intersection (in the inside of the block) with a red dot. Then, throw the block. In general, it will rotate or tumble in the air, but the red dot will move in a smooth curve through space. This smooth curve, describing the translation motion, can be mathematically defined as a parabola, and it can be shown that no matter how the block rotates or tumbles, the red dot will always move in a smooth parabola. Furthermore, the particular parabola in any experiment is always determined by the velocity and position of the red dot at the time of release of the block by the thrower. (The velocity of any body is defined as its speed and the direction in which it is moving, so to specify velocity, you must give the speed, as, say 20mph, and the direction, say vertically, from the ground.)

One may object at this point and say: "But no, you are wrong! If I put forward or top spin on a tennis ball, the ball will plunge or dip down; if I undercut it (backspin) with the same stroke, the ball will rise. So clearly, the center of the ball cannot move in the same curve." Both observations are correct, for the motion of the tennis ball is determined by both the force of gravity and the effects of air moving relative to the ball, whereas for the tumbling block, the effects of air motion are relatively unimportant. Such is also the case of the Freestyler during aerial maneuvers, because the speed of flight is sufficiently slow and the irregu-

larity of his body is such as to make the effects due to air movement over the body negligible.

The red dot in the plastic block marks the center of mass (c.m.) of the block, which, for the case of motion near the surface of the earth, is the same as the center of gravity (c.g.). For symmetrical bodies of (essentially) even density, the c.m. can be readily located as the intersection of the axes of symmetry. Thus, as result of the throwing experiments, it can be concluded (and it is possible to demonstrate mathematically also) that, at least for one rigid, symmetrical block, the c.m. moves in a parabola, and that this path is not affected by any tumbling of the block.

The remarkable fact is that even when consideration is given to very complicated bodies that are joined together with hinges, pivots, etc., such as the human body, the c.m. of the entire assembly will again move in a smooth parabola, no matter how the body parts wiggle, rotate, fold, or bend relative to each other. (This conclusion holds if the only important force acting on the assembly is the force of gravity, and air resistance is negligible.) But the question now is, how does one define the c.m. of such an assembly of parts? Clearly, the argument used about axes of symmetry for the single block will not work. It can be shown that the c.m. can always be defined mathematically for any assembly of bodies, but for qualitative understanding, the simple case of two rectangular blocks hinged together, as shown in the two sketches below, must be considered. (For simplicity, the side view only is shown, rather than the three-dimensional picture.)

The c.m. of each body individually can be located by the symmetry of axes, say at m_1 and m_2 as shown. These locations will not change unless each body breaks up. Then, the c.m. of the combined body will always be on the line joining m_1 and m_2 as shown. So, if the composite body "jackknifes," the c.m. of the system may lie outside the body itself. It is also important to note that the c.m. of the system will lie closer to the heavier of the two. In particular, the product of the mass m_1 times the distance of m_1 from c.m. (d_1 or D_1) must always equal m_2 times its distance (d_2 or D_2) from the c.m. As the body parts move about, these distances will change. That is why the symbols d_1 and D_1 are used to express the distance of m_1 from the c.m. of the system.

Obviously, the addition of about 20 pounds of boots, bindings, and skis will have quite an effect on the location of the c.m. of the skier. For the "unequipped" upright human body, the c.m. will lie somewhere in the pelvic region. When all the gear is added, the c.m. moves downward. How far the c.m. moves will depend on the physical build of the skier (height, weight, etc.) and the equipment used.

The essential conclusion, then, is that the c.m. of the skier and equipment moves in a smooth parabola; rotational motion takes place about this smooth curve; and the body parts may be reoriented in any manner relative to this smooth curve by internal muscle actions. The path or trajectory of the c.m. is defined by the position and velocity of the c.m. at takeoff. Thus, the "flight path" of the aerialist is defined once and for all by the speed at the lip of the jump, the direction he is moving, and the shape of the jump. By extending his legs, or springing, the jumper can impart

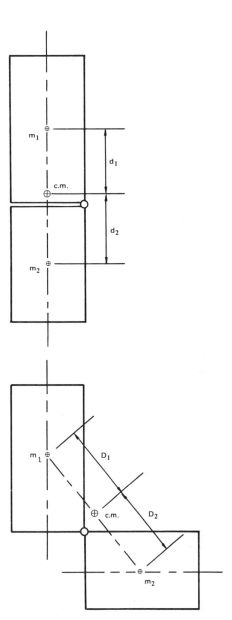

Fig. A-2

changes to some extent to the speed of the c.m. but mostly to the direction in which the c.m. moves just after takeoff. The primary determinant of his trajectory, however, will be the overall speed (as defined by his inrun), and the shape of the lip. Since the rotational motion or wiggling about of the body parts once the aerialist is airborne cannot alter the motion of the c.m., if he draws up or extends the legs in midair a compensatory movement of the upper body takes place. For example, if the legs are drawn in during an upright jump, the torso (or entire body) will seem to drop, as it should to keep the product m_1d_1 equal to m_2d_2. Conversely, extension of the legs from a bent position will cause the whole body to appear to rise.

The intricacies of rotational motion should be considered further. Again, for simplicity, first consider a single, rigid rectangular block as shown in Fig. A-1. The physical properties of such an object that are significant in analyzing the possible rotational motion it may undergo need to be defined. As is known from everyday experience, all bodies have mass, which is a measure of how much the body resists any change in its state of motion (when friction is eliminated, as in the case of a body resting on ice or frictionless rollers). The more massive the body, the harder it is to set into motion, and conversely, once moving, the harder it is to stop it from moving. This property is called inertia, the tendency of any body to resist changes in its state of motion.

The usual experience in this regard is with cars; the larger, more massive a car is the harder it is to accelerate or stop. Mass is an important property in the study of translation motion. However, the velocity with which it moves also plays an important part. The faster a body of given mass moves, the more force is required to change its state of motion. In physics, this phenomenon is expressed by Newton's Law of Motion, which identifies the property of momentum—the product of velocity and mass—as the determining characteristic of the body's motion. Newton's Law states that the amount of force exerted on the body is equal to the change of momentum in time.

For everyday applications of this law, the mass of the body is constant. The application of force results in a change in the velocity called acceleration. Note that the velocity may increase or decrease in magnitude (i.e., the speed changes) or the magnitude (speed) may stay the same and only the direction of the velocity may change. Any change in velocity is an acceleration; an example of constant speed but changing direction is experienced when rounding a curve in a car at a constant 55mph. The results of acceleration (change in the direction of the velocity) are experienced by the passengers of the car as centrifugal force. The skier experiences a centrifugal force whenever he makes a turn. The more carved the turn is (minimum decrease in speed), the more centrifugal force is felt.

Consideration can be given to the rotational motion of the block in Fig. A-1 in analogy to the translational motion. The property analogous to the mass is now called the moment of inertia, the property of a given body that measures how much the body resists changes in its rotational state or, simply, changes in its state of spin. The larger the moment of inertia, the harder a body is to spin up or to stop. Of course, when rotation or spin is spoken of, there is an implicit assumption of a center of spin or axis of rotation. Therefore, the moment of inertia of the body must be calculated for the center of spin and the appropriate spin axis. For example, if the body is free to move in space, the center of spin is the center of mass; if the body is suspended by one point as, say, a boxing bag, the center of spin or rotation is the point of suspension. For all Freestyle aerial applications, the center of spin will always be the c.m. of the body, and the axis of spin or rotation some axis through the c.m.

The magnitude of the moment of inertia depends on the mass distribution of the body. To illustrate, in a barbell with (equal) weights attached to the ends, the moment of inertia about the c.m. (a point midway between the weights) can be increased by adding more weight at the ends. The moment of inertia, can also be increased while keeping the total weight exactly the same, by simply extending the length of the bar, that is, by placing the given weights farther from the c.m. In contrast to the property of mass, which typically cannot be changed once all the gear is on, the moment of inertia of the human body can be changed by movements of the limbs and torso. The moment of inertia about our c.m. can be increased by extending the body, and decreased by contracting or rolling up into a tight tuck. The addition of 20-plus pounds of gear at the end of the feet allows more drastic changes in the moment of inertia than those possible for the "unequipped" body. For this reason, some gymnastic or trampoline movements are quite difficult to transfer to Freestyle aerials.

As a consequence of the above, the moment of inertia of the body (for simplicity, visualize the block in Fig. A-1) will, in general, be different for each of the axes of symmetry: longitudinal, lateral, and frontal. For the human body, with no equipment, in the upright position, the moment of inertia about the longitudinal axis (essentially parallel to the spine) will have the least value, that about the frontal axis the maximum value, and that about the lateral axis an intermediate value. This fact has some interesting consequences. But first the analogy of rotational motion to the translational motion should be considered somewhat further.

Just as in the case of translational motion, the velocity of the body was important in defining momentum, so also would the rate of spin or rotation, or angular velocity, play an important role. The product of the moment of inertia and the angular velocity is called the angular momentum. Applying Newton's Law of Motion, the time rate of change of the angular momentum of a body can be deduced to be equal to the applied external moment (or torque or twisting force). That is, to change the angular momentum, a torque or moment must be applied to the body; if no moment acts, then the angular momentum will remain constant.

Rotations about the c.m. must be considered, because that is the one (mathematically identifiable) point whose motion can be readily calculated. (Recall that the c.m. moves in a smooth parabolic arc or flight path independent of the rotational motion of the body.) Moments or torques are measured relative to the c.m., as is the moment of inertia.

The following three experiments can be carried out with your rectangular block (you can actually try these with a block of wood to better understand what happens). Throw the block into the air, each time imparting rotation about each of the three axes as shown. The only effective force acting on the block in midair will be gravity—if the block is fairly heavy and spins relatively slowly, the effects of air can be neglected. Since gravity acts equally on all parts of the body, it can exert no twisting torque or moment on the block. Thus, since all moments are zero after the block is in the air, the total angular momentum of the block will remain a constant. As you carry out the experiments, notice that for the cases A-3-1 and A-3-2 the body seems to continue to spin essentially about the axis you started it spinning about, even if you were fairly careless when throwing the block up, "careless" meaning that some amount of spin or rotation about the other two axes is also imparted. For case A-3-3, however, note that no matter how carefully you try to have it spin only about the lateral axis, the block rapidly develops rotation about the other axes! That is, not only does it somersault (the desired motion), but it also twists and tips, a fairly general tumbling motion. This remarkable behavior can be shown (again, by the mathematical "magic" and Newton's Laws) to depend on the relative magnitudes of the moments of inertia about the three axes. That is, spin about the axes with minimum and maximum moment of inertia (cases A-3-1, A-3-2) is stable—small rotations introduced about the other axes stay small—but the spin about the axis of intermediate value

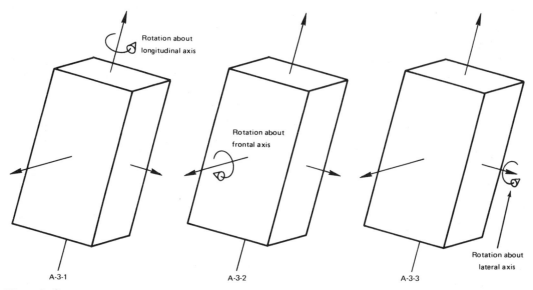

Fig. A-3

of the moment of inertia is unstable —small rotations about either of the other two axes will grow large. You may well ask at this point, "But how can the spin about these other axes grow, and the angular momentum—defined as the product of moment of inertia and angular velocity—remain constant?" The answer is of course that the angular momentum involves all the moments of inertia and spins about all the axes; as spin about, say, the longitudinal axis, grows, spin about the initial axis of rotation must decrease in just the right amount. In order to fully understand this phenomenon, try coloring the faces of your wooden block in different colors and carefully observe what happens as you toss it in the air with different initial rotations.

The implications of the above observations for aerials are now obvious. If one considers layout Front and/or Back Somersaults with a twist, then the above applies directly. The somersaulting axis (lateral) of the human body is the axis of intermediate moment of inertia. To have a clean somersault in the layout position with no twist or tipping sideways is quite difficult, and requires a precise, balanced takeoff—one must spring evenly

off both feet, move arms symmetrically, and not introduce any sideways lean. On the other hand, a layout with a twist can be accomplished by introducing a fairly small amount of initial twist about the body's longitudinal axis, or by tipping sideways about the frontal axis. Initial twist about the longitudinal axis will keep the feet and head in roughly the same plane throughout the Twisting Somersault. Tipping sideways will cause the feet and head to move out of the principal plane of motion as the twisting action takes place.

Up until now, rotation of a single body such as the rectangular block or the human body has been looked at in a single, upright position. However, because the human body acts as a collection of (essentially) rigid links joined together at the joints, some interesting changes in rotational motion can occur during flight. The first possibility is changing the moment of inertia about each of the three axes while in flight. For example, the moment of inertia about the lateral or somersault axis can be decreased considerably by assuming a tight tuck position. Thus, since the total angular momentum of the body must be a constant once in the air (recall that there are no torques or moments acting after the aerialist leaves the lip of the takeoff), a decrease in the moment of inertia requires an appropriate increase in the spin rate or speed of rotation. The device of controlling the rate of spin about any of the three body axes by changing the moment of inertia about that axis is widely used by Freestylers to correct body position for landing, etc. In this regard, note that the effect of the skis, boots, and bindings—the weight of this equipment attached to one extremity of the body—will have substantial effects on the moment of inertia about the lateral and frontal axes. That is, for a given initial spring, the rotation rate in the layout position will be substantially slower for the equipped body than for the unequipped. Similarly, the change in spin upon tucking will be different for the two cases. For this reason, after practice of the maneuvers on the trampoline and/or diving board, the aerialist will still have to make substantial timing adjustments for all Inverted Aerials when going on the snow with full gear.

Recognition of the above facts will enable a Freestyler to intelligently select gear and analyze difficulties encountered in performing certain stunts. As a general rule, if Twisting Somersaults give problems, they can be made easier (quicker twists) by selecting short, light skis with low swing weight. Also, aligning the skis somewhat with the longitudinal axis of the body will decrease the moment of inertia about that axis, making twists faster. The inverse is also true—if the jumper consistently twists more than desired, a longer, heavier ski will slow him down.

The last topic to be covered under rotational motion deals with so-called action-reaction twisting in the air. In general, it is true that if one part of the body twists or rotates in one direction, another part must twist in the opposite direction to compensate. For example, if the upper body twists to the right during an upright aerial, the lower body (and skis, boots, etc.) must twist to the left. Therefore, once in the air, a complete twist of the body (a 360-degree rotation about the longitudinal axis) cannot be initiated by upper or lower body rotation about that axis. Similarly, if no somersaulting action (rotation about the lateral axis) is initiated as the jumper leaves the takeoffs, none can be started by bending at the waist, etc.

However, the fact that the human body has four pivoted appendages—the arms and legs—allows self-rotation to take place in the air without the aid of any external moments, and without violating the conservation of angular momentum law. A detailed description, as well as mathematical analysis, of the mechanics of self-rotation is contained in the articles by Kane and Scher, and Kane, Headnick, and Yatteau, cited below. The principal findings will be briefly described here.

Consider first the problem of initiating a somersault in the air, that is, initiating a rotation about the body lateral axis. Such a rotation can be initiated by moving the arms symmetrically in a conical fashion relative to the body. This motion is illustrated in Fig. A-4, where the body is abstracted as the familiar rectangular block and the arms represented by two sticks pivoted at the shoulder with weights at the ends. If the arms are moved symmetrically in a conical fashion as shown, the body will rotate in the opposite direction about the lateral axis. The arm motion cone axis must be in the plane formed by the lateral and longitudinal axes, but may be tipped downward with respect to the lateral axis (shown parallel in the sketch for ease of visualization). The cone angle—the angle between the cone axis and arm—is restricted by the physiological nature of the shoulder joint. Rotation of the body, then, is in the opposite sense to the rotation of the arms. That is, if the arms move "forward" on the cone as shown, a "backward" rotation of the main body is initiated. So, in order to help or augment a forward somersault,

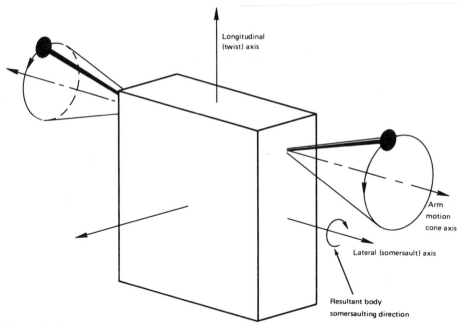

Longitudinal
(twist) axis

Arm
motion
cone axis

Lateral (somersault) axis

Resultant body
somersaulting direction

Fig. A-4

the arms must circle backwards, and vice versa. The amount of somersaulting action possible this way will depend upon how well the maneuver is carried out and whether the body is in a layout or tuck position. The moment of inertia in the tuck position is slightly less than half that in the layout for the human body, so roughly twice as much rotation of the main body per cycle of arm motion is possible in the tuck. With the arms straight out (cone axis parallel to the somersault axis), on the average 12 degrees of somersault rotation per arm cycle in the layout and 24 degrees in the tuck position are possible. Somewhat more rotation per cycle is possible if one lets the cone angle increase to about 60 degrees and drops the cone axis 30 degrees down from the lateral axis.

Side somersault action can be similarly initiated by an arm coning action, except that now the arm cone axes are aligned parallel to the frontal axis (i.e., the arm motion cone axis swings 90 degrees forward in Fig. A-4). The general conclusion is the same: a side somersaulting action can be initiated opposite to that of the arm motion. Because one is

now attempting to initiate rotation about the axis of maximum moment of inertia for the body, the amount of side somersault rotation per cycle of arm motion is limited to less than 16 degrees. Slight improvement may be gained by tucking the legs and decreasing the moment of inertia somewhat.

The last self-rotation action (about the longitudinal or twist axis) may be performed with either leg or arm movements, or both in conjunction. The nature of the motion for the legs in Fig. A-5 is illustrated. If a typical cycle is traced, starting from position 1 with, say, the right leg forward and left back, the legs are rotated in a conical fashion, as shown, to position 2. Typical cone angles might be on the order of 30 degrees. Then the legs are moved in a line under the body back to their original positions. During the coning motion from position 1 to 2, the body rotates (twists) to the left as shown; during the motion from position 2 to 1, the body rotates to the right. However, there is a net rotation to the left. Typically, values on the order of 70 degrees of twist per leg cycle can be obtained, when no boots or skis are con-

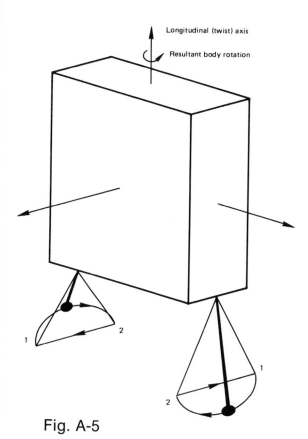

Longitudinal (twist) axis

Resultant body rotation

Fig. A-5

sidered. Addition of the mass of the equipment at the extremities would substantially improve this value—just how much has not been quantitatively determined. During the leg cycle, the toes point forward, so this maneuver in conjunction with a Helicopter could be utilized to achieve a "Helicopter Split Daffy."

The degree to which the self-rotation maneuvers described may be effective for the Freestyle aerialist is still largely unknown. Experimentation with body movements under controlled conditions will show which movements are useful and in what capacity—initiating, assisting, completing, or "saving" Twisting Aerials. Until the questions are better explored, the best way to ensure that a Twisting Somersaulting Aerial is completed is to initiate the correct motions on the lip of the jump.

All of the possibilities of aerial maneuvers and what physics dictates should take place have been examined qualitatively. Although no demonstrations in the strict sense were presented to prove certain points, all the maneuvers described can be mathematically described, the conclusions verified, and the general features quantified. A selected set of references has been included for those interested in further study.

NEUROMUSCULAR CONTROL OF MOVEMENTS†

Since muscles respond only as a result of nerve impulses, it is important to understand how the nervous system acts and to what degree conditioning and practice influence it. Nerve impulses travel in two directions—from the sensory mechanisms of the body which provide the senses of touch, taste, smell, sight, hearing and muscle/joint awareness (kinesthetic sense) to the brain and from the brain to the various functional mechanisms of the body. These impulses may be perceived on the conscious level or unconscious level. The nervous system is composed of an infinitely large number of possible impulse pathways; these nerve impulse pathways are inherited and vary from individual to individual. Coordinated and skillful movements are the result of complex physiological processes resulting in properly sequenced and timed nerve impulses. Along with other physical capabilities, the nervous system matures with age and is not capable of the full range of operation until maturity. Thus the immature nervous system of small children will hamper speedy and precise impulse patterns and hence intricate movements. Since maturity is ill-defined and the rate at which it is achieved varies from child to child, it is extremely difficult to give guidelines as to when full capacity is to be expected. We do have gross manifes-

† Reproduced from *Biomechanics Manual*, J. Vagners. Published by the Professional Ski Instructors of America, Denver, Colorado, 1972, with the author's permission.

tations resulting in the classification as "slow learners" and "fast learners."

Several measures of neuromuscular control are important:

reaction time: The time interval between stimulus and beginning of response.

reflex time: The time interval between stimulus and beginning of automatic reflex response (this is the same as reaction time *only* for automatic or innate reflexes).

movement time: Time to accomplish the task.

The reaction time for all voluntary movements directed by the brain is usually composed of reflex time plus thought or analysis time by the brain and is a measure of the lag in the functions of the nervous system. Reflex time can be improved somewhat through specific tasks; the majority of improvement occurs in thought or analysis time. As thought time decreases, the involvement of the conscious brain becomes less and less as the specific analysis patterns are relegated to lower levels of the brain. The final leveling-off time is achieved when a movement becomes a "conditioned reflex" and conscious thought is used only to amplify or diminish the learned reflex.

The most important innate (inborn) reflexes for movement analysis are:

stretch reflex: This is a gravity-conditioned reflex to maintain upright position of the body and to maintain body alignment. An example of this reflex is the head snap or jerk one experiences when falling asleep in a sitting position with the head unsupported.

extensor reflex: This is again a gravity-conditioned reflex activated by pressure on the bottom of the feet resulting in extension of all weight-bearing joints. Its importance lies in maintaining balance and shock absorption when load is increased such as in jumping, etc.

withdrawal reflex: This is primarily a pain or perceived pain condition reflex such as occurs upon touching a hot stove.

Innate reflexes can be augmented by conscious movements or overridden.

Of primary concern to the teacher and coach is the nature and development of conditioned reflexes. A guiding principle is that skill is attained at the highest level when the reaction approaches reflex time with diminishing conscious thought involvement-conditioned reflex. Thus the importance of developing kinesthetic sense from the very start is evident. As noted before, the nerve pathway possibilities are inherited but the full development depends on practice. Nerve impulses establish preferred pathways in the central nervous system through repetition of travel—wear a rut with diminished resistance along the rut. As the rut becomes well-worn, conscious involvement of the brain decreases.

As a general practice, key gross maneuvers and movements and skills should be learned first and then more refined skills brought in. When the body encounters new situations, and they are in some sense similar to familiar situations for which a conditioned reflex has been established, it will react according to the conditioned reflex in combination with the appropriate innate reflex. Overriding by conscious involvement will depend upon the performers thought or analysis time in relation to the time available in the new situation. To train the analysis process properly for a maneuver which is to be of general utility in a given aspect of skiing, the maneuver should be practiced under all anticipated conditions. For example, skiing all types of terrain and snow conditions for the recreational skier and running as many different slalom courses and combinations as possible for the racer. Many runs over the same course or same type of course are detrimental. To decrease analysis time, a keen kinesthetic sense must be developed, primarily with respect to snow, terrain and speed variations. One means of improving a specific sensing capability is to isolate it from input from the other senses—for example sight and sound. Isolation allows one to concentrate on the information from the desired sense.

It is apparent that considerable thought must be devoted to the development of a training program for all Freestyle events. In particular, the selection of exercises, both on the snow and off, is extremely important. We recommend practice of all of the "gym" exercises discussed in this text because they have been carefully thought out in terms of specific benefit for specific maneuvers. Do not try them a few times, find that you can do them successfully and therefore forget to practice the "dryland" exercises. To continually improve your performance on snow, develop and carry out the exercise program described throughout the ski season as well as off-season. In addition, to improve body awareness and kinesthetic sense, we recommend participation in modern dance classes and/or ballet classes whenever the opportunity arises.

THE BALANCE MECHANISMS AND BODY EQUILIBRIUM

Successful skiing at all levels requires that the body be in stable equilibrium —at balance with all acting forces and moments. The process of maintaining equilibrium when the body is moving involves the input from the sensing mechanisms and appropriate muscular adjustments. The sensing mechanisms are:

the semicircular canals of the inner ear: These fluid-filled canals are arranged in three perpendicular planes and sense rotation about any axis.

the otoliths (ear stones) of the utricle (located in the vestibule): These calcium deposits on fine hairs act as accelerometers and measure changes in linear acceleration.

visual: Direct and peripheral vision provides important clues to the body orientation.

kinesthetic sense: The proprioceptors of the nervous system provide information about the relative positions and movements of various body parts. Information about acceleration, speed and orientation is also obtained from sensing pressure changes on the skin (face, bottom of the feet, etc.).

These sensing mechanisms can be confused by various means. First, all have sensing thresholds: slow rotations, gradual accelerations and slow, smooth movements will not be sensed without visual input. In addition, shock loads and vibration will confuse the input signals to the brain, hence the importance of minimizing head movements in all maneuvers. Fatigue will dull the senses since the nerve impulses will be impeded—this fact becomes critical when performing complicated, intricate movements at high speeds. The joint movements utilized to shift the center of gravity and body parts in response to perceived disturbances provide invaluable information about equilibrium via the kinesthetic sense. Immobilizing a joint will decrease sensitivity—as with neck braces and high, stiff boots. High, stiff boots work in two ways to decrease the amount of kinesthetic information from the lower extremities: (a) they decrease ankle mobility, placing a greater burden on the muscles of the lower back, abdomen, and upper legs; and (b) they decrease the feel of the bottoms of the feet for changes in pressure distribution and shock loads. Involvement of large muscle groups in maintaining balance decreases and complicates the initiation of small corrective adjustments involving minor muscle groups. (Superposition of fine movements on gross movements requires very intricate nerve impulse patterns because of possible conflicting nerve pathway requirements.)

Stable body equilibrium may be classified as statically or dynamically stable. Static stability is accomplished when the c.m. of the stationary body lies within the base of support. It is enhanced by lowering the c.m. toward the base of support and/or by widening the base of support. Thus we drop the body, use wide stance and wedge to enhance stability. Dynamic stability is the result of an intricate interplay of external forces, effects of accelerations, and internally generated body movements. For slow maneuvers, one is primarily concerned with force and linear acceleration effects, hence the basic concepts from static stability apply. For fast movements—particularly if ballistic movements are involved—the effects of angular momentum and external moments become critical. For advanced skiing, angular momentum—moment balance about the center of mass—is the primary consideration. Enlarging the base of support for fast maneuvers is feasible up to a point—use of wider stance than is dictated by the individual's body structure, use of wedge, etc.—but is finally inhibiting because lower-body mobility is decreased. For dynamic stability, flexibility and mobility of all body segments are critical. Lowering the center of mass is beneficial in reducing the moment arms of external forces (snow on skis), but excessive collapsing of the body reduces mobility if large muscle groups are in contraction to maintain low position.

GLOSSARY

anticipation or anticipate: Twisting the upper body in the direction of the intended turn or spin in order to lead the turning skis; or allowing the legs and skis to complete a turn or preturn while the upper body leads the lower body into the next turn. Both methods stretch or lengthen the muscles primarily responsible for turning the legs and skis. This preliminary movement, which stretches the muscles before initiation of the turn, increases the potential for a stronger muscular contraction to help turn the legs and skis.

axis, frontal: This is the front-to-back axis, around which aerialists do Side Somersaults. It is as if an imaginary pole enters the chest and passes out through the back.

axis, lateral or side: This is a side-to-side axis around which aerialists somersault. It is as if an imaginary pole passes through the body entering at the right hip and passing through the left hip.

axis, vertical or longitudinal body: This is the up-and-down axis around which Freestylists twist or do 360 Spins. It runs from the head to the feet.

balance: Steadiness, a condition of not falling over in any direction.

banking: Tipping the body to the inside of a turn to counteract centrifugal force and to maintain balance and edging.

biomechanics: The study of body motion, which includes the knowledge of classical physics (specifically dynamics), kinesiology, and anatomy. In actual application, biomechanics of skiing deals with the whole skier, his body and mind, the skis, boots, poles, and snow.

blind: A condition during a maneuver in which the performer does not see the landing area until contact or just a moment before. A blind maneuver allows little time for major corrective movements to assure proper landing.

camber: The arched curve that is built into a ski and is apparent when it lies unweighted on a flat surface. Camber distributes the skier's weight along the entire running surface of a ski.

carving or carved turn: A turn primarily caused by an edged ski cutting a curved track in the snow. A ski must be bent into a reverse camber shape and have side cut in order for the carving action to take place. In a "Pure Carved Turn," there is no skidding. The ski leaves a track in the snow no greater than its width. The radius of a "Pure Carved Turn" is limited by the degree to which the ski can be bent into reverse camber. Hence, it is usually a long radius turn. In short radius carved turns, some slipping occurs. Usually the tails slide out if there is increased forward pressure. One speaks of a carved turn if the edge ski is primarily responsible for the turn. A skidded turn by comparison is usually initiated and controlled primarily by muscular action.

center of gravity: An imaginary point around which the body weight is equally distributed. This can vary according to body build and body position. Also, varying the location of the extremities will change the location of the center of gravity. Generally, it is located in the hip/pelvis area near the navel, but can also fall outside of the body. For example, when somersaulting in a pike position, the center of gravity can be somewhere in the space between the upper body and legs.

centrifugal force: A force that tends to push any rotating object outward away from the center point of its curved path. Skiers moving in a straight line will feel the pull of this force when turning. Skiers usually counteract its effects by leaning to the inside of the turn to remain balanced.

coming-out: Extending the body to slow rotation and spinning in preparation for a landing or completion of a maneuver.

edge-set or checking: Increasing the bite of edges on the snow. An edge-set may reduce a skier's speed as the ski is bent into greater reverse camber. Setting the edges also allows a more forceful snapping of the ski into its original shape when pressure is eliminated by absorption or rebound. This action of the skis assists unweighting and change of edge. Other uses of an edge-set or check are to create a stable platform from which to unweight, or to place the muscles in a more favorable position to contract when initiating a rotary turning force. An edge-set can be initiated by a quick dropping in the ankles and knees, displacement of the tails of the skis at an angle to the original direction of travel, and increasing the bite of the edges on the snow. The same effect can be accomplished by tightening the turning radius so reverse camber is increased before unweighting.

edging: The angle at which a ski may be rolled onto its edge. Edging can be caused by a lateral movement of the ankles, knees, hip, or torso. The degree of edging affects the lateral slipping movement of the ski. Additional edging in a turn increases reverse camber and usually decreases side slipping.

fall-line: The line a freely moving body would follow down a slope if influenced only by the pull of gravity.

focus point: Something a Freestyler is intensely looking for near the completion of a maneuver. Focusing on an object helps to stop the turning of the head in the direction of movement and helps slow the turning of the body. It is also used to establish one's relative body position in rotary and twisting movements. The focus point is usually a prominent object.

Freestyle skiing: A newly created sport consisting of three events: Mogul skiing, Stunt and Ballet, and Aerial Acrobatics. Competitors are evaluated on the skills they demonstrate, their degree of proficiency, and the difficulty of the maneuver.

Hot Dog skiing: A slang term to describe reckless, wild skiing in which the participant is frequently on the brink of disaster.

inside edge–outside edge: Refers to the edge of the ski in relation to the center line of the body. When a person stands on both skis pointing straight ahead, the inside edges of the skis are adjacent to each other. This identification of inside or outside edge does not change at any time during spins, crossovers, etc.

inside ski–outside ski: Refers to the position of the skis in relation to the other ski while in a turn. The outside ski is away from the direction of the turn.

kinesthetic sense: An awareness of body position and movement both of body parts relative to each other and of the entire body relative to its surroundings. The sensory receptors of the nervous system provide information about the relative position and movements of various body parts. Information about acceleration, speed, and orientation is also obtained from sensing pressure changes on the ski, face, bottom of the feet, neck muscles, and other body parts. A kinesthetic feeling for a stunt occurs when it has been practiced so many times that the muscles develop an almost automatic response when performing the maneuver.

leverage: Pressure on the ski caused by the action of the skier or changes in terrain. Pressure can vary along the length of the ski as a result of moving the skier's center of gravity. The changing of the center of gravity is felt by the changing pressure along the sole of the foot. Feeling more weight on the ball of the foot will increase the pressure toward the front of the ski; increasing weight on the heel of the foot will move the pressure toward the tail of the ski. Varying the weight along the sole of the foot causes a variation of the point at which the ski assumes its greatest deflection in the reverse camber position. As a result, the ski will turn differently according to where pressure is applied along its length.

looking: Leading a twisting movement of the body by turning the head and looking in the direction of the turn or spin; or concentrating on locating a focus point during a stunt.

lost: To be unaware of one's body position during a maneuver, usually caused by a failure to find a focus point. It is a very unpleasant and dangerous experience.

mogul: A bump on the hill usually carved out of the snow by the cutting action of ski edges.

momentum: (1) Impetus resulting from movement; (2) the force with which a body moves, the product of its mass and its velocity.

peripheral vision: Side vision; having to do with the outside boundary of vision that is to either side of direct sight.

pressure: The amount of weight or downward force applied to the ski. It can vary by shifting weight along the sole of the foot, standing on the ski, changing edging and centrifugal force in a turn, by muscular action, and/or changes in terrain.

proprioceptors: Sensory receptors in the muscles, tendons, and joints that feed information to the high brain centers concerning tension of muscle fiber, joint angles, and position of the body part being moved (Rasch and Burke).

ready position: A position in which the body is ready to move quickly in any direction with maximum speed, characterized by keeping the center of gravity over the feet and maintaining slight flexion in the joints. This position differs from a relaxed stance in which the skeleton carries most of the body weight by aligning bones over bones in a supporting position.

reverse camber: Bowing the ski opposite to its natural arch. In reverse camber the ski bends down from the tip and tail to a maximum deflection under the skier. Reverse camber in part determines the arc of a carved turn. Eliminating the skier's weight on the ski allows it to snap back to its original shape, aiding in unweighting.

rising–sinking motions: Slow movements of the body to change position or to adjust for balance.

roll: A somersault done on the snow. The head is tucked to the chest and the body rolls across the snow.

skating step: Pushing off the inside edge of the outside ski (in relationship to a turn) and stepping onto the outside edge of the inside ski to accelerate, transfer weight, and change direction.

skill: Proficiency or ability gained by practice and/or knowledge. In skiing it refers to learning the coordinated body–ski movements of balancing, turning, skidding, carving, absorbing, etc.

Snowsnake: An infrequently seen, although commonly felt, white snake that attacks skiers by a lightning fast coiling of its body around the victim's legs, causing a stumble or fall. Although its identity has not been positively confirmed, many skiers attest to its existence.

somersault or flip: A roll done in the air. The skier usually starts on his feet and rolls over in the air landing on his feet without touching any part of his body to the snow during the maneuver.

spotter: The person standing by, spotting the performer.

spotting: (1) Watching another performer and being ready to help or protect him in the event of his miscalculation or mistake during a maneuver. (2) Looking for a landing area or focus point.

traverse: Crossing the hill at an angle to the fall-line.

twist: Rotating on the vertical or longitudinal body axis. The upper body or legs can be twisted to help the skis turn. In Aerial Acrobatics a twist can be a complete rotation around the long body axis or legs can be rotated against a stable upper body.

unweighting: Reduction or elimination of the skier's weight on the snow.

up–down motion: Quick vertical body movements, usually to initiate unweighting.

uphill ski–downhill ski: Refers to the position of one ski in relation to the other ski while in a traverse position on a hill or traversing.

weight transfer: Transfer of body weight from one ski to the other.

wide track: Skis and feet comfortably separated in a parallel position but no wider than hip-width apart.

wind-up: A turning of the body opposite to the direction of the intended action. It is used to prepare for a more forceful initiation of a stunt.

wrap: An action of the arms being drawn in close to the body to speed twisting rotation.

BIBLIOGRAPHY

Abraham, Horst. *American Teaching Method.* Vail: The American Ski Instructors Educational Foundation, Professional Ski Instructors of America, 1974.

Batterman, Charles. *The Techniques of Springboard Diving.* Cambridge: The MIT Press, 1968.

Campbell, Stu. *Ski With the Big Boys.* New York: Winchester Press, 1974.

Cooper, Dr. Kenneth H. *Aerobics.* New York: Bantam Books, 1968.

Griswold, Larry and Glenn Wilson. *Trampoline Tumbling Today.* Second edition. New York: A. S. Barnes and Company, 1970.

Joubert, Georges. *Teach Yourself To Ski.* Trans. Sim Thomas. Aspen: Aspen Ski Masters, 1970.

Joubert, Georges and Jean Vuarnet. *How To Ski the New French Way.* Trans. Sim Thomas and John Fry. New York: The Dial Press, 1967.

LaDue, Frank and Jim Norman. *This Is Trampolining.* Cedar Rapids: The Torch Press, 1956.

Logan, Gene A. and Wayne C. McKinney. *Kinesiology.* Los Angeles: William C. Brown Company, 1970.

Maltz, Maxwell. *Psycho-Cybernetics.* Englewood Cliffs: Prentice-Hall, 1960.

PNSIA Examination Guide for Freestyle Certification. Seattle: Pacific N.W. Ski Instructors Association, 1974.

Rasch, Philip J. and Roger K. Burke. *Kinesiology And Applied Anatomy.* Second edition. Philadelphia: Lea and Febiger, 1963.

Vagners, Dr. Juris. *Biomechanics Manual.* Denver: Professional Ski Instructors of America, 1972.

Witherell, Warren. *How The Racers Ski.* New York: W. W. Norton and Company, 1972.

BIBLIOGRAPHY FOR APPENDIX

Arnold Sommerfeld. *Mechanics,* Vol. 1 of Lectures on Theoretical Physics. New York: Academic Press, 1964.

George W. Housner and Donald E. Hudson. *Applied Mechanics: Dynamics.* New York: D. Van Nostrand Co., 1959.

Richard P. Feynman. *The Feynman Lectures on Physics,* Vol. 1. Reading, Mass.: Addison-Wesley Publishing Company, 1963.

E. N. Simons. *Mechanics for the Home Student.* London: Sliffe and Sons Ltd., 1950.

T. R. Kane and M. P. Scher. "Human Self-Rotation By Means of Limb Movements," *J. Biomechanics,* Vol. 3, pp. 39–49 (1970).

T. R. Kane, M. R. Headnick, and J. D. Yatteau. "Experimental Investigation of an Astronaut Maneuvering Scheme," *J. Biomechanics,* Vol. 5, pp. 313–320 (1970).

INDEX

Boldface Numbers Refer To Illustrations

211